The Rose of Sharon Block Book

WINNING DESIGNS FROM THE EQ6 CHALLENGE

SHARON PEDERSON

Martingale®
& COMPANY

The Rose of Sharon Block Book:
Winning Designs from the EQ6 Challenge
© 2010 by Sharon Pederson

 *Martingale®*
& COMPANY

That Patchwork Place® is an imprint
of Martingale & Company®.

Martingale & Company
20205 144th Ave. NE
Woodinville, WA 98072-8478 USA
www.martingale-pub.com

Printed in China
15 14 13 12 11 10   8 7 6 5 4 3 2 1

**Library of Congress Cataloging-in-Publication Data
is available upon request.**

ISBN: 978-1-60468-011-9

Mission Statement

Dedicated to providing quality products
and service to inspire creativity.

Credits

President & CEO: Tom Wierzbicki

Editor in Chief: Mary V. Green

Managing Editor: Tina Cook

Developmental Editor: Karen Costello Soltys

Technical Editor: Robin Strobel

Copy Editor: Marcy Heffernan

Design Director: Stan Green

Production Manager & Text Designer:
Regina Girard

Illustrator: Laurel Strand

Cover Designer: Stan Green

Photographer: Brent Kane

Dedication

To the memory of my dear friend and mentor,
Dorothy Nylin, 1921–2009.

Contents

Preface

This book was the brainchild of Elizabeth Phillips, my business partner and friend. In the spring of 2008, Elizabeth, her husband, Chris Manuel, and I formed a company called Nine Patch Media, which produces instructional DVDs for quilters. We've had the pleasure of working with some of North America's most popular quilting teachers, and Elizabeth has come up with ideas about the best way to promote each teacher's work.

While we were shooting the DVD to accompany my latest book (*Machine Appliqué for the Terrified Quilter*, Martingale & Company 2008), she suggested that the homemade freezer-paper template I was using for my Rose of Sharon quilt (it's called "Xs and Os" in the book) would be a useful tool for my students if it was professionally made out of template plastic. Before I knew it, we had a lovely bright-orange template to offer. As her mind never stops, before I knew it, that innocuous little template grew and grew into the incredibly successful Rose of Sharon Block Challenge.

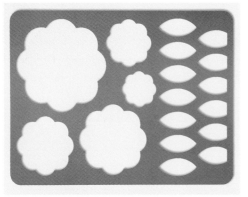

The orange template that started it all.

Elizabeth is the queen of "what if." What if we have a contest to design Rose of Sharon blocks using your template? What if we work with Electric Quilt to make the block shapes available on their website? What if we design a die to use on the AccuQuilt machine to cut out not only the freezer-paper templates but also the fabric? What if we work with Island Batik to provide the most beautiful fabric to make the blocks? What if the blocks could be digitized by Oklahoma Embroidery Supply and Design (OESD) and done on an embroidery machine? And, what if we support a charity in the process?

And so the Rose of Sharon Block Challenge was born. Not only are our partner companies supporting our vision to bring the best in appliqué design to quilters everywhere, with products and tools that make creating spectacular quilts fun and easy, but many of them are helping the Alzheimer's Art Quilt Initiative (AAQI) to raise awareness of Alzheimer's and to raise funds for Alzheimer's research. The Rose of Sharon products and partners are:

- The *Rose of Sharon* book that you are holding in your hand from Martingale & Company
- The *Rose of Sharon* DVD from Nine Patch Media
- The Rose of Sharon dies for the AccuQuilt Studio and GO! cutters
- The *Rose of Sharon* CD of embroidery designs from OESD
- The Rose of Sharon fabric collection from Island Batik, Inc.

The 850-plus blocks that were submitted inspired us with their beauty and ingenuity. There were only three shapes available to use, but that didn't slow our winners down. Our judges, Ricky Tims and Alex Anderson, whittled down the vast number of blocks to a dozen, and then I also got to design a block to make the 13-block quilt you see on the cover. But there were so many great entries, that we just had to share more of them with you.

With the wonderful embroidered blocks digitized by OESD, and the blocks they appliquéd on the new Bernina 830 machine, I had the pleasure of making a few smaller samples as well.

We hope you enjoy creating your very own Rose of Sharon project, be it a quilt, table runner, wall hanging, or whatever you choose. We also hope that you'll send us pictures of the finished project. We'll post them on our website (www.sharonpederson.com or www.ninepatchmedia.com) for all the world to see— and if you feel you'd also like to support the Alzheimer's Art Quilt Initiative, information about how to make a donation to them is listed in the "Resources" section on page 91.

Happy quilting,

Sharon Pederson

Introduction *by Ami Simms*

My mother made a left-hand turn from the left-hand turn lane—except there wasn't one. She put on her blinker, slid across the yellow line, and slowly eased to a stop. There we sat on the wrong side of the road, facing the wrong way, waiting for traffic coming at us at 50 miles an hour to "clear," so she could complete her turn. Looking back, that was one of the first signs that something was wrong. I had heard of Alzheimer's but didn't really know what it was. I just thought Mom made a really poor driving decision, vowed none of us would ever ride with her again, and tried to stop screaming.

By the time Mom was diagnosed with Alzheimer's and had moved in with us, she was starting to lose her nouns. Proper names blinked in and out of her memory, and she began to name things with words that started with the same letter (pan for pin) or rhymed (moth for cloth). Sometimes she'd correct herself, sometimes not. "Thingy," "whatsit," and "whozy" invaded every sentence.

Once a gourmet cook, now she couldn't identify food. The differences between a sprig of broccoli and a French fry were no longer apparent to her.

She sewed bits of patchwork almost every day for me. Everyone needs to feel needed and productive, but over time her memory could no longer help her wind the bobbin or thread the machine. I remember coming in to help her, and there she was with her Bernina tipped over on its back. She was attempting to thread the machine from the bottom. She eventually forgot how to sew altogether.

As the disease progressed, the world around her became more and more frightening, filled with things and people she couldn't identify or understand. She began to see things that weren't there and, understandably, became agitated and frightened. Her sense of humor and good nature, which had prevailed for so long in spite of what Alzheimer's had taken from her, gave way to episodes of rage and paranoia. When I could no longer take care of her, I moved her into an Alzheimer's facility. She never understood why. Every day, for an entire year, she begged me to take her home.

Over the next two years her world became increasingly smaller; she became more confused. Most meaningful language left her. We communicated through music, humming and singing together. Eventually Mom lost every memory she ever had, every skill she ever learned, and every relationship she ever held dear. She had no memory of the past, no way to imagine the future, and she lived totally in the moment. Some moments were good, others not so much.

My mother lost the ability to care for herself in almost every way imaginable. She even forgot how to sit. She had to be cued verbally and physically to approach the chair, feel it on the back of her legs, put her hand on an arm rest, bend her knees, and move her body down. Had I not experienced this disease with her, I could never have imagined it. Mom died in my arms seven years after being diagnosed with Alzheimer's.

I've been a quilter since the late '70s. Quilting is my vocation, my avocation, my passion, and the reason my house is always such a mess. I've got thread in my veins. In 2005, shortly before my mother moved into the Alzheimer's facility, I got it into my head that I needed to make a quilt about Alzheimer's, to share what I was going through as a caregiver. It would be a very ugly quilt, with lots of angry black thread pounded into a top of mismatched seams, puckers, and holes. I didn't have time to sneeze, let alone make a new quilt, yet the idea festered. I floated it in front of some of my professional colleagues, who suggested, kindly, that nobody would want to see a quilt about Alzheimer's, at least not if it looked like that!

In the process I discovered that they were probably correct, but more importantly, that I was not the only quilter on the planet who had a family member or friend with Alzheimer's. One idea for a very ugly quilt grew to an entire exhibit of extraordinarily beautiful and poignant quilts about Alzheimer's that would both honor and remember those who had forgotten themselves, as it comforted those who loved them, and educated people who had never experienced Alzheimer's in their families. "Alzheimer's: Forgetting Piece by Piece" began traveling in August of 2006 and has been seen by more than 223,000 people at 49 venues in 31 states. A new traveling quilt exhibit called "Alzheimer's Illustrated: From Heartbreak to Hope" will begin touring the United States in 2011.

Influenced by generations of quilters before me who have used needle and thread for good works, and by Virginia Spiegel's wildly successful effort to turn quilted postcards into cash for the American Cancer Society, I had created the Priority: Alzheimer's Quilt Project earlier in 2006. Priority: Alzheimer's Quilts are small-format quilts with a maximum size of 9" x 12". The project was named both for the USPS priority mailer into which the little quilts must fit without folding, and for the hope that quilters would make the struggle to find a cure for Alzheimer's a personal priority. Priority: Alzheimer's Quilts are donated by quilters and auctioned online or sold outright. Together these two projects comprise the efforts of the Alzheimer's Art Quilt Initiative, now a national nonprofit charity run totally by volunteers. All profits fund Alzheimer's research.

By participating in a hobby that we love, quilters and quilt lovers are giving hope to an estimated 26 million individuals worldwide who have this vile disease.

I am so grateful to Sharon Pederson and Elizabeth Phillips for envisioning the Rose of Sharon Project as one that would not only serve the quilting community with projects, patterns, designs, fabric, and tools centered around a time-honored and beloved quilt block, but also as one that creates an opportunity to serve the greater good through corporate philanthropy. I am thrilled that the Rose of Sharon partner companies are helping to spread the word about the Alzheimer's Art Quilt Initiative and supporting our mission of raising awareness and funding research through art.

Thank you!

Ami Simms

Founder & Executive Director
Alzheimer's Art Quilt Initiative
www.AlzQuilts.org

How to Use This Book

The blocks in this book are the winning entries of an online block challenge, which was held in October and November of 2009. The challenge was to design a Rose of Sharon block using only three given shapes in limited sizes. Quilters from 11 countries entered, and the 12 winning blocks represent 5 countries! If you have Electric Quilt 6 (EQ6 as it's affectionately known) on your computer, you can go to electricquilt.com and download the Rose of Sharon project files and design your own blocks. EQ has made them freely available to anybody who has the program.

I had the honor of turning the winning blocks into the quilt on the cover, and those plus other amazing block entries, totaling 83 blocks, are offered here for your use.

I also got to play with the beautiful embroidered blocks provided by OESD, and the pillow and wall hanging were made with them.

If you want to make the cover quilt the same way I did, then all the directions you need are between these covers. However, you always have the option of doing your quilt in whatever way you find pleasing. Choose fewer blocks and make a table runner or wall hanging. Add more blocks and make a king-size quilt. One of the wonderful things about quilting is that there are so many ways to do it—and the way *you* choose is the right way.

In 2002 my first book, *Reversible Quilts: Two at a Time*, was published. In it and the subsequent book *More Reversible Quilts* (Martingale & Company, 2004), I explained how I make my quilts. By breaking the quilt down into blocks that are pieced, sometimes appliquéd, and then layered and quilted before being joined to the next block, you eliminate the need to baste your quilt. The technique takes a lot of the drudgery out of quilting and reduces the amount of handling needed to finish. That is how this quilt was put together. So, before you get too much farther ahead I would strongly recommend you read "Quilting 101" on page 85. If you decide, after reading that section, that you would rather make your quilt the conventional way (joining the blocks and sashing, and then layering, and basting) I will assume that you know how to do that. As with every other aspect of quilting, the way *you* prefer to do something is the *right* way to do it.

My preferred methods of appliqué are all machine techniques, but that does not mean *you* must also do them by machine. The patterns are all here, and whatever method you choose for making them is entirely up to you. But, for those of you who would like to appliqué them by machine, and who would also like a little direction as to how to go about it, I offer my approach. Please feel free to take whatever information you find useful and employ it while leaving the bits that don't appeal behind.

The Rose of Sharon block has been around for many years and was often made as a gift for a bride. Because they were "best" quilts, which were carefully stored, many examples of early Rose of Sharon quilts have survived. They were often made in the popular mid-1850s color scheme of red, green, and white, but contemporary versions are seen in every color of the rainbow.

One characteristic of many of the variations of the Rose of Sharon block is the scalloped blossom piece. This shape is one of the three that were provided for the block challenge that produced all of the blocks in this book. See page 90 for the patterns.

I'm sure that the creative genius of many quilters out there could have come up with some awesome designs using more complicated pattern pieces, but what good are they if only a handful of people could ever make them? We wanted these designs to be accessible. So, let's just jump right in and start—and of course if you want to add other shapes, it's your quilt, so you just go right ahead and add them.

Enjoy.

The Rose of Sharon
Block Challenge Quilt

Roses of Remembrance

Finished size: 63" x 63"

MATERIALS

Blossoms, Leaves, Circles, and Stems

It's impossible to predict fabric choices, and therefore yardage amounts, for the appliqués. If you want to make a quilt similar to mine, I can tell you that with a long quarter yard each of 18 different fabrics (see "Challenge Fabrics from Island Batik, Inc." on page 92), I was able to make not only this quilt, but also two four-block table toppers and a three-block wall hanging. I had to get more of one green fabric—making lots of bias stems used up more than my original ¼ yard—but I have quite a bit of some of the other fabrics left over.

If you'd prefer to use fewer than 18 appliqué fabrics, you'll probably need more than ¼ yard of each.

So, I'll leave it up to you to decide how much you'll need for your blossoms, leaves, circles, and stems. For recommended yardage for the background, sashing, borders, binding, and backing fabrics, read on.

Background, Sashing, Borders, Binding, and Backing

All yardages are based on 42"-wide fabric.

3⅜ yards of fabric for block backgrounds*

2⅛ yards of fabric for sashing, borders, and binding for the front of the quilt

1⅝ yards of fabric for sashing and borders for the back of the quilt

3⅜ yards of fabric for backing*

2½ yards of 96"-wide batting

Freezer paper or 4½ yards of 18"-wide fusible web

If your fabric does not have at least 42" of usable width, you'll need 4⅓ yards.

CUTTING

From the fabric for background, cut:

- 13 squares, 14" x 14"*
- 2 squares, 11" x 11"
- 2 squares, 22" x 22"

Squares are cut large to give you something to hold onto when quilting and to allow for "take-up" if heavily quilted.

From the fabric for sashing, borders, and binding on front of quilt, cut:

- 13 strips, 2½" x 42" (sashing)
- 7 strips, 2½" x 42" (borders)
- 7 strips, 2½" x 42" (binding)

From the fabric for backing, cut:

- 13 squares, 14" x 14"
- 2 squares, 11" x 11"
- 2 squares, 22" x 22"

From the fabric for sashing and border on back of quilt, cut:

- 20 strips, 2½" x 42"

From the batting, cut:

- 13 squares, 14" x 14"
- 2 squares, 11" x 11"
- 2 squares, 22" x 22"

CREATING THE BLOCKS

Starting on page 15, photos of the 13 blocks used in this quilt are shown at half size, in the fabrics used by each block's designer. Below the block photo, you'll find the number of templates needed, the stitching order, and assembly tips. You can substitute any of the blocks from "More Beautiful Blocks" (starting on page 31) for the blocks in your quilt.

To make each block, follow these steps.

1. Using the template patterns on page 90, trace and then cut out the number of templates required for your block. When tracing, you can use freezer paper for invisible machine appliqué (see page 75), fusible web for fused machine appliqué (see page 82), or a combination of the two.

2. Create guides for placing the appliqué pieces in one of the following ways.

   Photocopying: Take this book to a photocopying center and enlarge the block photo by 200%. (Alternatively, if your home printer will print a 12" block and you have a scanner, scan the photo and then print a 200% enlargement.) If you use blocks from "More Beautiful Blocks," enlarge the images 300%. Use this full-size enlargement as a placement diagram. First draw a 12" square on the right side of the background fabric with a washable marker. To position the fabrics, put the placement diagram on a light box, with the background fabric on top.

Basting: Lightly draw a 12" square on the wrong side of your 14" background fabric. The square marks the perimeter of your finished block. Now draw lines dividing the block in half vertically, horizontally, and diagonally.

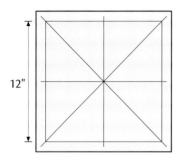

With a neutral thread in your machine, stitch over the drawn lines with a basting stitch. Although not as easy as putting a full-sized picture on your light box and lining pieces up on top, basted guide-lines do give enough coordinates to position the appliqué pieces on the background. Measure the placement of motifs on the block photos, multiply by two (remember the photos on pages 15–28 are shown at half size), and then use the measurements and basting lines to guide your placement of the appliqué motifs. If you are substituting a block from "More Beautiful Blocks," multiply the measurements by 3. When you're finished appliquéing the block, remove the basting threads.

3. Appliqué the blocks, referring to "Invisible Machine Appliqué" on page 75 or "Fused Machine Appliqué" on page 82 as needed.

4. Layer each block with backing and batting and quilt as desired. Trim each block to 12½" x 12½".

Quilting on back of Block 11. See the complete back of the quilt and its quilting on page 14.

Corner and Side Triangles

Our quilt blocks are on point, so after you've finished appliquéing, quilting, and trimming the 13 blocks, you'll then have to appliqué, quilt, and trim the eight side triangles and the four corner triangles.

1. From the background fabric, cut the 11" squares in half once on the diagonal for the four corner triangles. Repeat with the 11" backing and batting squares.

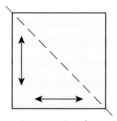

Corner triangles.
Grain is on two short sides
of triangle.

2. From the background fabric, cut the 22" squares in half twice on the diagonal, which will produce the eight side triangles. Repeat with the 22" backing and batting squares.

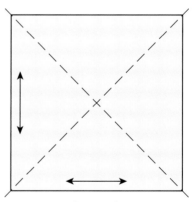

Side triangles.
Grain is on long edge of triangle.

3. With a washable marker, draw a line ¾" in from the edges of the three sides of the corner triangle and 1" in from the edges of the side triangles. Be sure to center your appliqué inside these lines.

4. After appliquéing and quilting, you must trim the outside edges of the triangles. Trim to ¼" beyond the lines you drew in step 3. At this point, I trim only the long side of the corner triangles and the two short sides of the side triangles. Don't worry about the outer edges of your triangles being untidy. Once the quilt is sewn together, you'll square up the four corners and trim the outside edges.

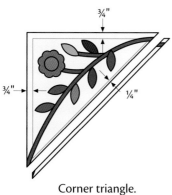

Corner triangle.
Trim long side.

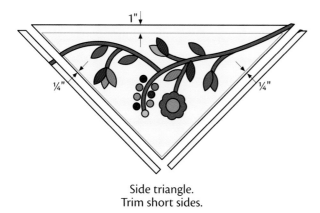

Side triangle.
Trim short sides.

QUILT ASSEMBLY

1. Referring to the photograph on page 10, arrange the blocks, side triangles, and corner triangles in diagonal rows. Following the instructions in "Sashing" on page 85, sew the blocks and side triangles into rows. Quilt the sashing as you go. Trim the sashing flush with the blocks.

2. Join the rows to the sashing, remembering to align the sashing strips where they meet; again, quilt the sashing as you go.

3. Sew the sashing to the last block on each corner and trim all of the sashing flush with the side triangles.

4. Find the center of the sashing strip and a corner triangle. Align the two centers and sew the corner triangle on. Repeat for the other corners.

5. With a long ruler, tidy up the edges of the quilt, being careful to maintain a 90° angle at the four corners.

6. Referring to "Terre's Borders" on page 87, add borders and quilt as desired.

7. Referring to "Basic Binding" on page 88, add binding to your quilt.

I love making reversible quilts, and if you follow the quiltmaking directions as written, that's what you'll end up with. On the reverse side of my quilt, Barbara Shapel's multicolored quilting shines against dark blue backing fabric. I used the same sashing and border fabric on both sides of my quilt, but you could choose different fabrics for each side if you'd like dramatically different looks for the front and back.

The Winning Blocks

During the development stage of the Rose of Sharon Block Challenge, my partner Elizabeth and I tried to figure out a way to have one of our blocks end up in the quilt. Obviously we couldn't enter the Challenge. The solution to our problem was to have 12 blocks chosen from the challenge entries and our block would become the thirteenth one needed to finish the quilt.

So, a drum roll please, here they are—the 12 winning blocks in the Rose of Sharon Block Challenge. These were chosen by Ricky Tims and Alex Anderson from the 50 blocks that made the short list. Then we added our block. Thanks again to Ricky and Alex for taking on the difficult task. It was a hard one, believe me.

BLOCK 1

Designed by Simonetta Marini, San Giovanni, Persiceto, Bologna, Italy

Cutting

Blossoms: 4 red A; 4 blue B, 1 bluish green B (5 total B); 4 red C; 1 red D

Leaves: 8 green A, 8 dark green B, 8 bluish green D

Circles: 8 gold A, 1 gold B

Bias stems: 96" of light green, 20" of gold

Stitching Order

1. Appliqué the center blossoms, starting with D, followed by B. Top with circle B.

2. The eight D leaves will be covered by the bias stems, so it's not necessary to turn leaf edges under. Iron the freezer-paper templates to the *right* side of the fabric and cut them out without adding a seam allowance. On the wrong side of the fabric, put a small amount of Liquid Stitch around the edges and glue the D leaves in place. Remove the freezer paper.

3. Position the green stems and glue in place, leaving any area unglued where a stem, either green or gold, crosses under it. Position the gold stems; then sew all the stems down.

4. Stitch eight leaf A, then four blossom A, then four circle A.

5. In each corner, appliqué two leaf B topped by a blossom C, a blossom B, and a circle A.

BLOCK 2

Designed by Judy Best, London, Ontario, Canada

Cutting

Blossoms: 4 burgundy B, 1 orange B (5 total B); 3 red D, 1 orange D, 1 black-and-red D (5 total D); 1 dark gold E

Leaves: 4 blue A; 3 light green C, 4 bluish green C, 3 green C, 3 dark green C, 3 blue C, 3 red C, 1 orange C (20 total C); 1 green D, 4 bluish green D, 1 light green D, 1 dark green D, 1 blue D (8 total D)

Circles: 4 gold B, 1 green-and-yellow B (5 total B)

Bias stems: 4 green, 1½" each; 4 green, 4" each (22" total)

All but the largest leaves at the corners are on the Rose of Sharon die for the AccuQuilt GO! machine.

Stitching Order

1. Sew all bias stems.

2. Center flower: Stitch blossom E, then one D, then the orange blossom B, topped by circle B.

3. Middle flowers: Appliqué four of blossom D, then four burgundy blossom B, and four circle B.

4. Outer flowers: Stitch 3 red and 1 orange leaf C (buds) and eight outer D leaves, then 16 of leaf C, removing the freezer paper as you go.

5. Appliqué four of leaf A around the center flower.

17

BLOCK 3

Designed by Dianne Gronfors, Bracebridge, Ontario, Canada

Cutting

Blossoms: 8 red B, 4 orange C, 1 red D, 4 red E, 1 black-and-red F

Leaves: 8 green A; 6 dark green B, 4 bluish green B, 6 green B (16 total B)

Circles: 8 black-and-red B, 5 gold C

Bias stems: 8 bluish green, 4" each (32" total)

Straight stems: 4 bluish green, 3½" each (14" total)

Stitching Order

1. Appliqué all stems.

2. Sew the center eight leaf B (partially covered by center blossom).

3. Stitch all of the blossoms from largest to smallest, then all of the circles.

4. Finish with the remaining eight leaf B, and all eight of leaf A.

BLOCK 4

Designed by Elizabeth Phillips, Courtenay, British Columbia, and Sharon Pederson, Black Creek, British Columbia, Canada

Cutting

Blossoms: 1 blue D, 1 orange G, 1 blue I, 1 black-and-red K

Leaves: 12 various colors half-leaf B for buds, 24 bluish green leaf B

Bias stems: 8 green stems, 2" (16" total)

Straight stems: 4 green, 2½" each (10" total)

Stitching Order

1. Appliqué all the stems.
2. Stitch all blossoms from largest to smallest.
3. Sew all of half-leaf B in various colors.
4. Sew all remaining leaf B.

BLOCK 5

Designed by Leslie Collins, El Granada, California,
United States

Cutting

Blossoms: 4 orange B, 4 red C, 1 orange C (5 total C);
4 burgundy D; 1 red F; 1 burgundy G

Leaves: 4 gold A, 4 burgundy B, 8 bluish green C,
8 green D

Circles: 4 gold A, 4 burgundy A, 4 black-and-red A
(12 total A); 8 blue B; 1 black-and-red C

Straight stems: 16 pinkish brown, 1½" each (24" total)

Stitching Order

1. Appliqué stems.

2. Stitch blossoms from largest (G) to smallest (B),
   then circle C and A.

3. Appliqué leaf D, followed by leaf C, and then leaf B,
   followed by leaf A.

4. Finish with remaining circles.

BLOCK 6

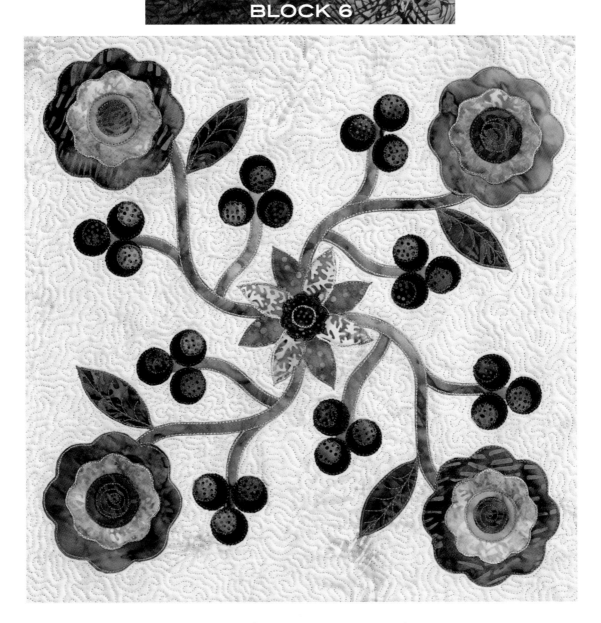

Designed by Jo Moury, Haymarket, Virginia, United States

Cutting

Blossoms: 1 pinkish brown A; 4 gold C; 2 red E, 2 blue E (4 total E)

Leaves: 4 orange A, 4 gold A (8 total A); 4 green B

Circles: 1 bluish green A, 24 pinkish brown A (25 total A); 24 burgundy B; 4 blue C; 2 red D; 2 bluish green D (4 total D)

Bias stems: 4 green, 5" each; 4 green, 3" each; 4 green, 2" each (40" total)

Stitching Order

1. Appliqué all stems, starting with the 2" ones, followed by the 3", then the 5".

2. Center flower: First sew 4 orange leaf A, and then the gold leaf A, then blossom A, and finally circle A.

3. Corner flowers: Appliqué blossom E, blossom C, then circle D, then circle C.

4. Add the B and A circle clusters, making sure they cover the stem ends.

5. Sew the four B leaves.

BLOCK 7

Designed by Rebekah Reinheimer, Jerusalem, Israel

Cutting

Blossoms: 1 blue C*, 2 red D, 1 red F, 1 orange G

Leaves: 4 orange A, 2 bluish green A, 4 blue A (10 total A); 3 blue C, 1 bluish green C, 2 black-and-red C (6 total C); 1 red D, 2 blue D, 2 orange D (5 total D); 1 blue F

Circles: 2 gold A, 10 black-and-red A, 14 orange A, 22 red A (48 total A); 2 black-and-red B; 2 black-and-red C; 2 gold D

Bias stems: 2 bluish green, 4" each; 2 bluish green, 5" each; 2 bluish green, 6" each; 2 blue, 9" each (48" total)

Straight stems: 1 green, 2½"; 1 green, 4½" (7" total)

Stitching Order

1. Appliqué bias stems from the base of the block up.

2. Sew the two straight stems.

3. Center flower: Stitch the blossoms from largest to smallest. Blossom C* does not have the edges turned under. Add the four orange leaf A pieces centered around blossom C.

4. Appliqué two blossom D, followed by all the circles from largest to smallest.

5. Top flower bud: Sew one red leaf D, then two black-and-red leaf C, followed by two orange leaf D.

6. Finish with the remaining leaves.

* *You can substitute a circle the size of Blossom C.*

BLOCK 8

Designed by Suzy Prickett, Melbourne, Florida, United States

Cutting

Blossoms: 1 bluish green E, 1 orange H

Leaves: 8 green A, 8 red A (16 total A); 4 red B, 8 bluish green B, 8 green B (20 total B)

Circles: 12 gold C, 1 red D

Bias stems: 4 burgundy, 2½" each (10" total)

Straight stems: 4 burgundy, 3½" each (14" total)

Stitching Order

1. Appliqué bias stems followed by straight stems.

2. Sew blossom H, then blossom E.

3. Appliqué all of the circles.

4. Corner buds: Stitch the four red leaf B, and then the eight bluish green leaf B.

5. Sew the remaining red and green leaves.

BLOCK 9

Designed by Barb Vlack, Saint Charles, Illinois,
United States

Cutting

Blossoms: 1 orange C, 4 red C (5 total C);
1 black-and-red E

Leaves: 8 blue A, 8 green B, 4 bluish green C, 4 bluish
green D

Circles: 4 orange A, 5 pinkish brown B, 28 assorted
colors B for corners (33 total B)

Straight stems: 4 bluish green, 3" each (12" total)

Stitching Order

1. Appliqué all stems.

2. Sew the four leaf D, and then the four leaf C on top
of leaf D, followed by the four circle A.

3. Stitch blossom E, and then the five blossom C.

4. Sew all the circle B.

5. Appliqué all leaf B, and then all leaf A.

Designed by Candace Door, Sidney, Nebraska, United States

Cutting

Blossoms: 4 orange B, 4 blue B (8 total B); 1 gold E; 1 light green H; 1 burgundy K

Leaves: 4 orange D; 4 burgundy E, 8 green-and-yellow E (12 total E)

Circles: 4 gold B, 4 bluish green B (8 total B); 4 blue C; 1 blue D

Bias stems: 4 burgundy, 2" each; 4 burgundy, 3" each (20" total)

Stitching Order

1. Stitch the 2" stems, and then the 3" stems.

2. Appliqué the burgundy leaf E, and then the eight green-and-yellow leaf E. All of the leaves in this block are partial, so you have to finish only one end.

3. Sew four orange leaf D, and then the four blue circle C.

4. Appliqué all of the blossoms, from largest to smallest, and then the remaining circles.

BLOCK 11

Designed by Pat Daniels, Winnipeg, Manitoba, Canada

Cutting

Blossoms: 1 orange B, 4 red B (5 total B); 5 gold C; 1 red D, 4 dark gold D (5 total D)

Leaves: 24 red A, 4 gold A, 12 dark gold A, 8 yellow-and-green A, 4 green A, 4 dark green A, 4 blue A (60 total A); 8 light green B

Circles: 4 burgundy A, 1 black-and-red B

Bias stems: 8 green, 2" each; 4 pinkish brown, 3½" each; 4 bluish green, 4½" each; 4 blue, 4½" each (66" total)

Stitching Order

1. Appliqué the 3½" stems that lead to the four corner blossoms, and then the four blue leaf A hidden under the 4½" stems.

2. Sew the eight 4½" stems, then the 2" stems.

3. Stitch the eight leaf B in the center.

4. Appliqué all of the blossoms from largest to smallest, followed by all the circles.

5. Buds: Sew leaf A in the center, then the partially covered leaf, then the top leaf. The three leaves form a bud overlap, so remove the freezer paper as you go. In the outer buds the bottom piece extends farther than the inner buds.

6. Appliqué the eight remaining leaf A.

BLOCK 12

Designed by Claudia Chang, Taipei, Taiwan

Cutting

Blossoms: 4 red C, 1 blue E, 1 red H

Leaves: 4 red A, 8 blue A, 20 light green A (32 total A)

Circles: 32 orange A, 4 gold C, 1 gold D

Bias stems: 4 green, 2½"; 4 green, 3½"; 4 green, 6½"
(50" total)

Stitching Order

1. Stitch all bias stems from shortest to longest.

2. Appliqué all blossoms, from largest to smallest.

3. Buds: Appliqué four red leaf A, and then eight blue leaf A.

4. Sew the light green leaves, and then all of the circles.

BLOCK 13

Designed by Kari Bauer, Oak Park, Illinois, United States

Cutting

Blossoms: 5 red A; 4 orange B; 1 orange C, 4 gold C (5 total C); 4 red D; 1 gold E; 1 red G

Leaves: 12 assorted blue and green A; 8 bluish green B; 8 dark green D

Circles: 8 blue A, 5 black-and-red A (13 total A)

Bias stems: 8 dark gold, 2" each; 4 bluish green, 9¼" each (53" total)

Stitching Order

1. Appliqué the 9¼" bias stems, and then the gold 2" bias stems.

2. Sew eight leaf D, forming the center. All leaf D are partial, so you only have to finish one end.

3. Stitch all of the blossom pieces from largest to smallest.

4. Sew all remaining leaves and all of the circles.

SIDE TRIANGLES

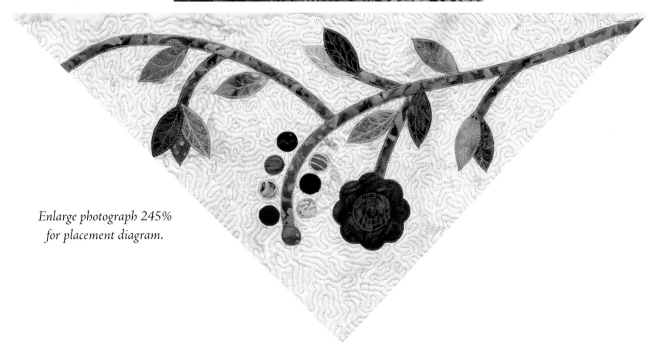

*Enlarge photograph 245%
for placement diagram.*

Designed by Elizabeth Phillips, Courtenay, British Columbia, and Sharon Pederson, Black Creek, British Columbia, Canada

Cutting

Amounts are for one side triangle. For eight side triangles, multiply each number by eight. The colors for the blossom, bud, leaves, and circles vary from triangle to triangle.

Blossom: 1 C

Leaves: 1 bud A, 11 assorted blue and green A
  (12 total A)

Circles: 8 assorted A; 1 C for center of blossom

Bias stems: 3 green 2", 1 green 3", 1 green 9", 1 green 13"
  (31" total)

Stitching Order

1. Start with the three 2" and one 3" bias stems. Next sew the 9" stem that has the stem with the bud attached, and then add the remaining 13" piece.

2. Appliqué the blossom, and then all of the circles.

3. Sew the bud's partial leaf followed by all remaining leaves, making note of where leaves overlap and remembering to remove the freezer paper from the bottom leaves before adding the top leaf.

CORNER TRIANGLES

Enlarge photograph 175% for placement diagram.

Designed by Elizabeth Phillips, Courtenay, British Columbia, and Sharon Pederson, Black Creek, British Columbia, Canada

Cutting

Amounts are for one corner triangle. For four corner triangles, multiply each number by four. The colors of the blossom, leaves, and circle vary from triangle to triangle.

Blossoms: 1 C

Leaves: 7 assorted blue or green A

Circles: 1 C

Bias stems: 1 green 2", 1 green 2½", 1 green 13"
     (17½" total)

Stitching Order

1. Appliqué the bias stems from shortest to longest.

2. Sew the blossom, followed by the circle.

3. Stitch the leaves.

More Beautiful Blocks

As you can imagine, there were lots of incredibly beautiful blocks remaining after we chose the winning blocks, and I want to share as many of them with you as I can. I've chosen my favorites and offer 70 of them here, so you have 83 blocks to choose from when making your projects! The names of the designers are listed, and what you're seeing is the Electric Quilt picture. I hope to make many of them up in the beautiful Island Batik fabrics, so please visit www.sharonpederson.com to see what I've done with them. Again, we thank the talented designers who shared their creations with us.

The block illustrations are 4" square. To make a 12" placement diagram, enlarge the illustration 300%.

BLOCK 14

*Designed by Mabel Reedijk-Pullen,
Dordrecht, Netherlands*

Cutting

Blossoms: 5 gold C

Leaves: 10 bluish green F

Circles: 5 orange C

Bias stems: 5 green, 2½" each (12½" total)

BLOCK 15

*Designed by Mabel Reedijk-Pullen,
Dordrecht, Netherlands*

Cutting

Blossoms: 7 green-and-yellow A; 3 red C,
1 orange C, 1 black-and-red C, 1 gold C,
1 dark gold C (7 total C)

Leaves: 7 burgundy A, 7 pinkish brown A (14
total A); 7 dark green E; 7 bluish green F

Circles: 7 blue A

Bias stems: 7 green, 3" each (21" total)

BLOCK 16

Designed by Pat Daniels,
Winnipeg, Manitoba, Canada

Cutting

Blossoms: 4 green-and-yellow A, 4 gold B,
4 red C, 1 dark gold K, 1 bluish green L

Leaves: 4 green A, 4 dark green A, 4 burgundy
A, 4 pinkish brown A, 8 orange A (24 total
A); 4 orange B, 4 red B, 8 blue B (16 total B)

Bias stems: 4 dark green, 5" each; 4 light green,
5" each (40" total)

BLOCK 17

Designed by Donna Krane,
Creston, British Columbia, Canada

Cutting

Blossoms: 1 gold C, 4 black-and-red D,
1 black-and-red G

Leaves: 4 green-and-yellow B, 12 dark green B
(16 total B); 4 dark green D; 4 green-and-
yellow F

Circles: 4 red A, 1 black-and-red C, 4 gold D

BLOCK 18

*Designed by Barbara Rodebush,
Galena, Missouri, United States*

Cutting

Blossom: 1 red C

Leaves: 16 orange A, 32 red A, 24 green A
(72 total A)

Circle: 1 dark gold B

Bias stems: 4 green, 9" each; 8 green, 2" each
(52" total)

BLOCK 19

*Designed by Susan Wood,
Shelley, Idaho, United States*

Cutting

Blossoms: none

Leaves: 11 gold B, 8 green B, 8 light green B,
27 orange B, 31 red B (85 total B)

Circles: 5 burgundy D

Bias stems: 4 dark green, 3½" each (14" total)

BLOCK 20

Designed by Nancy Rink,
Bakersfield, California, United States

Cutting

Blossoms: 2 dark gold D, 1 dark gold F, 1
 black-and-red H, 1 red J, 1 burgundy L

Leaves: 4 black-and-red A, 8 green B, 4 green C

Circles: 6 red B; 2 red D, 6 dark gold D
 (8 total D)

Bias stems: 4 green, 2½" each (10" total)

BLOCK 21

Designed by Simonetta Marini,
San Giovanni, Persiceto, Bologna, Italy

Cutting

Blossoms: 8 red A, 8 blue B

Leaves: 4 gold A, 8 pinkish brown A, 16 light
 green A (28 total A)

Circles: 8 gold A

Bias stems: 4 green, 2½" each; 4 green, 3" each;
 4 green, 4" each; 4 green, 13" each (90" total)

BLOCK 22

*Designed by Daphne Stewart,
Sunnyside, Washington, United States*

Cutting

Blossoms: 1 gold A, 1 burgundy A, (2 total A);
1 blue B; 1 orange C, 1 red C (2 total C);
1 red D; 1 red E; 1 orange F; 1 black-and-
red H

Leaves: 7 light green D, 4 dark green D,
5 bluish green D, 4 green D (20 total D)

Circles: 1 blue A, 1 orange A, 2 gold A, 3 red A,
1 burgundy A, 1 dark gold A (9 total A); 1
gold B

BLOCK 23

*Designed by Barbara Rodebush,
Galena, Missouri, United States*

Cutting

Blossoms: 2 red E

Leaves: 8 black-and-red A, 17 light green A
(25 total A); 4 red B

Circles: 2 gold D

Bias stems: 4 burgundy, 6" each (24" total)

Straight stems: 2 burgundy, 5½" each
(11" total)

BLOCK 24

Designed by René Barth,
Kewanee, Illinois, United States

Cutting

Blossoms: 2 pinkish brown A, 2 orange B,
   1 orange C, 1 burgundy D, 1 black-and-red
   F, 1 pinkish brown H

Leaves: 11 green A, 2 green B, 1 green C,
   1 green D, 8 gold C, 8 green-and-yellow D

Circles: 1 pinkish brown B, 1 orange C,
   1 burgundy D

Bias stems: 1 green 9", 1 green 7", 1 green 3½"
   (19½" total)

Straight stems: 1 green 3½", 1 green 2½"
   (6" total)

BLOCK 25

Designed by René Barth,
Kewanee, Illinois, United States

Cutting

Blossoms: 1 red D, 1 orange H

Leaves: 4 orange B, 8 red B, 8 green B, 16 gold
   B, 16 dark gold B (52 total B)

Circles: 1 gold D, 4 burgundy D, (5 total D)

Straight stems: 8 green, 2" each (16" total)

BLOCK 26

Designed by Vicki Willems,
Comox, British Columbia, Canada

Cutting

Blossoms: 3 orange B, 3 pinkish brown B
  (6 total B); 1 red C; 1 burgundy D,
  3 red D, 3 black-and-red D (7 total D)

Leaves: 4 dark green A, 4 light green A,
  3 bluish green A (11 total A); 2 dark green
  B, 1 green B, 3 bluish green B (6 total B)

Circles: 3 gold B, 3 dark gold B (6 total B);
  1 dark gold C

Bias stems: 6 green, 5" each (30" total)

BLOCK 27

Designed by Vicki Willems,
Comox, British Columbia, Canada

Cutting

Blossoms: 1 gold B, 1 burgundy B, 2 red B,
  3 black-and-red B (7 total B); 1 blue C;
  3 orange D, 4 gold D (7 total D); 1 red E

Leaves: 7 green A, 7 blue C, 7 bluish green D

Circles: 7 green-and-yellow A, 1 dark gold B

BLOCK 28

Designed by Simonetta Marini,
San Giovanni, Persiceto, Bologna, Italy

Cutting

Blossoms: 2 blue A; 1 blue B, 2 red B (3 total
  B); 1 red C

Leaves: 5 gold A, 10 dark green A, 10 red A
  (25 total A)

Circles: 2 gold A, 1 gold B

Bias stems: 2 green, 10" each; 4 red, 3" each;
  1 red, 13½"; 1 red, 14½"; 1 blue, 4½";
  1 blue, 5½"; 1 blue, 6"; 1 blue, 7"; 1 blue,
  9½"; 1 blue, 11" (103½" total)

You will also need three 3½" squares of pinkish
  brown under the small heart shape.

BLOCK 29

Designed by Simonetta Marini,
San Giovanni, Persiceto, Bologna, Italy

Cutting

Blossoms: 1 blue B, 1 blue E, 1 red H

Leaves: 8 green A, 16 bluish green A,
  12 dark green A (36 total A)

Circles: 1 burgundy B; 2 red C, 6 orange C,
  (8 total C); 4 red D

Bias stems: 81" total of assorted colors

BLOCK 30

*Designed by Jeanette Maiorano,
Springhill, Florida, United States*

Cutting

Blossoms: 1 pinkish brown A, 1 black-and-red
A, 2 gold A, 3 orange A, 2 red A (9 total
A); 1 gold B, 2 black-and-red B, 3 red B
(6 total B); 1 red C, 1 green-and-yellow C,
1 pinkish brown C (3 total C); 1 gold F,
1 orange F, 1 black-and-red F (3 total F)

Leaves: 7 green B, 7 dark green B (14 total B);
2 green C

Circles: 3 gold D, 3 bluish green D, 10 blue D
(16 total D)

Bias stems: 2 green, 1" each; 1 green, 1¼";
1 green, 1½"; 1 green, 2", 1 green, 2¼";
3 green, 4" each (21" total)

BLOCK 31

*Designed by Mary Markworth,
Nacogdoches, Texas, United States*

Cutting

Blossoms: 1 red C, 1 dark gold D, 1 red E

Leaves: 4 blue B

Circles: 1 green-and-yellow A, 40 assorted red,
orange, gold, dark gold, black-and-red, and
bluish green A, (41 total A); 1 burgundy C

Straight stems: 4 light green, 3" each
(12" total)

BLOCK 32

Designed by Scarlett Rose,
Anderson, California, United States

Cutting

Blossoms: 8 gold A, 4 orange B, 5 red C

Leaves: 16 dark green A, 8 green B, 4 dark
green C

Circles: 4 gold A, 5 gold B

Bias stems: 4 bluish green, 1½" each;
4 green, 6" each (30" total)

BLOCK 33

Designed by Scarlett Rose,
Anderson, California, United States

Cutting

Blossoms: 1 orange G, 1 red I, 1 burgundy K

Leaves: 4 blue A, 4 blue B, 4 dark green C,
4 dark green E

Circles: 9 gold B, 36 green-and-yellow B,
(45 total B); 1 gold D

Straight stems: 1 green, 4½"; 3 green, 3½"
each; 6 green, 1¾" each (25½" total)

BLOCK 34

Designed by Mary Seay,
Pasco, Washington, United States

Cutting

Blossoms: 5 orange A; 2 black-and-red B,
3 dark gold B (5 total B); 2 dark gold D, 3
orange D (5 total D); 1 red E, 2 black-and-
red E, 2 pinkish brown E (5 total E); 1 gold
G; 1 black-and-red H; 1 gold J; 1 red L

Leaves: 3 light green A, 5 green A (8 total A);
3 light green B, 5 green B (8 total B)

Circles: 20 blue A

Bias stems: 8 bluish green, 3" each (24" total)

BLOCK 35

Designed by Tara Hovis,
Alma, Michigan, United States

Cutting

Blossoms: 4 blue A, 4 orange B, 5 red C, 1 blue
F, 1 black-and-red H

Leaves: 4 green A; 4 green B, 4 red B, 8 black-
and-red B, 8 pinkish brown B (24 total B)

Circles: 1 orange C

Bias stems: 8 green, 2½" each (20" total)

BLOCK 36

Designed by Marlene Oddie,
College Place, Washington, United States

Cutting

Blossoms: 2 background C, 4 gold C, 3 dark gold C, 2 orange C, 6 red C, 1 black-and-red C (18 total C)

Leaves: 5 green C, 5 dark green C (10 total C)

Circles: none

Straight stems: 1 burgundy, 2½"; 1 burgundy, 3½"; 3 burgundy, 4½" each; 2 burgundy 5" each; 4 burgundy, 7" each (57½" total)

BLOCK 37

Designed by Pat Daniels,
Winnipeg, Manitoba, Canada

Cutting

Blossoms: 1 dark gold D, 1 gold L

Leaves: 1 green-and-yellow A, 2 dark gold A, 2 red A, 2 background A, 5 burgundy A, (12 total A); 1 gold B, 3 burgundy B (4 total B); 1 gold C; 3 gold D

Circles: 2 blue A, 2 red A (4 total A)

Bias stems: 1 orange, 4"; 1 dark gold, 7½" (11½" total)

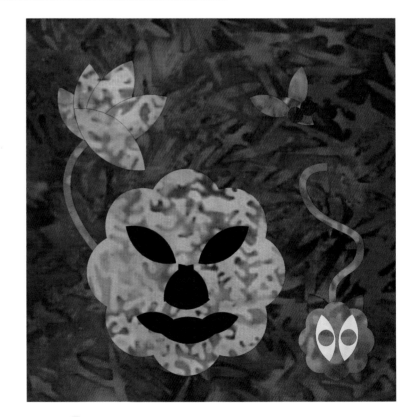

43

BLOCK 38

*Designed by Serena Toppins,
Branchland, West Virginia, United States*

Cutting

Blossoms: 4 orange C, 4 red D,
    4 black-and-red E

Leaves: 12 light green A, 12 dark green A (24
    total A); 4 orange B, 8 blue B (12 total B)

Circles: 4 gold C

BLOCK 39

*Designed by Sharon Simmons,
Brighton, Michigan, United States*

Cutting

Blossoms: 8 orange A, 1 dark gold B, 1 red C,
    1 dark gold F, 1 burgundy J

Leaves: 4 blue A, 8 green A (12 total A);
    8 bluish green B; 8 dark green C

Circles: 4 black-and-red A

Straight stems: 4 blue, 3" each (12" total)

BLOCK 40

Designed by Sharon Simmons,
Brighton, Michigan, United States

Cutting

Blossoms: 1 pinkish brown B, 1 red C, 1 gold
D, 1 red E, 1 gold I

Leaves: 4 blue A, 5 bluish green A, 4 green A,
4 dark green A (17 total A); 1 bluish green
B; 1 green C

Circles: 1 pinkish brown B, 2 burgundy C

Bias stems: 1 green, 9"; 1 green, 7½" (16½"
total or use satin stitch for stems)

BLOCK 41

Designed by Margaret Vachon,
Lancaster, California, United States

Cutting

Blossoms: 1 burgundy B, 2 red B, 2 gold B
(5 total B); 5 blue D; 1 burgundy F, 1 gold
F, 1 red F, 2 pinkish brown F (5 total F)

Leaves: 1 bluish green C, 1 light green C,
1 green C, 2 blue C (5 total C)

Circles: 5 red A, 5 pinkish brown A, 5 gold A
(15 total A); 5 orange B

Bias stems: 1 gold, 2½"; 1 green-and-yellow,
2½"; 1 green, 2½"; 1 blue, 2½"; 1 bluish
green, 2½" (12½" total)

BLOCK 42

*Designed by Ursula Barkau,
Bohmte, Germany*

Cutting

Blossoms: 4 red A; 1 gold B, 8 orange B,
(9 total B); 4 pinkish brown C; 8 black-
and-red D; 1 orange E; 1 red I

Leaves: 8 green A, 4 dark green F

Circles: 1 pinkish brown A, 4 black-and-red A,
8 gold A (13 total A)

BLOCK 43

*Designed by Ursula Barkau,
Bohmte, Germany*

Cutting

Blossoms: 1 orange A, 4 black-and-red A
(5 total A); 4 orange B; 1 pinkish brown D,
4 red D, 4 black-and-red D (9 total D);
4 pinkish brown E; 1 red H

Leaves: 8 green A, 8 dark green B

Circles: 4 orange A; 1 gold B, 1 orange B,
1 red B, 1 black-and-red B (4 total B)

Bias stems: 4 green, 3¼" each; 8 green, 1½"
each (25" total) or use satin stitch

BLOCK 44

Designed by Susan Arnold,
Sunnyvale, California, United States

Cutting

Blossoms: 1 burgundy D, 1 red H, 1 gold L

Leaves: 6 blue B, 6 bluish green B (12 total B);
3 red C, 3 burgundy C, 6 blue C, 6 bluish
green C (18 total C)

Circles: 6 dark gold D

BLOCK 45

Designed by Susan Arnold,
Sunnyvale, California, United States

Cutting

Blossoms: 4 gold C, 4 blue D, 1 gold H,
1 bluish green J, 1 light green L

Leaves: 8 green B, 8 dark green C

Circles: 4 light green B, 4 red C

Bias stems: 8 bluish green, 4" each (32" total)

47

BLOCK 46

Designed by Jo Moury,
Haymarket, Virginia, United States

Cutting

Blossoms: 2 dark gold A, 2 blue B, 2 red C

Leaves: 2 bluish green A, 2 blue A, 6 light green A, 4 green A, 2 dark green A (16 total A); 2 light green B

Circles: 2 orange A, 2 red A, 4 bluish green A, 4 dark gold A, 2 green-and-yellow A, 5 black-and-red A, 3 gold A, 2 blue A (24 total A); 2 blue B, 1 pinkish brown B, 2 burgundy B, 5 red B (10 total B)

Bias stems: 2 bluish green, 2" each; 2 green 6" each; 2 dark green, 14½" each (45" total)

Straight stem: 1 dark green, 7½"

BLOCK 47

Designed by Jo Moury,
Haymarket, Virginia, United States

Cutting

Blossoms: 4 orange B, 4 dark gold C

Leaves: 8 blue A, 8 light green A (16 total A); 4 gold B, 4 orange B, 16 green B, 8 dark green B (32 total B)

Circles: 4 blue A, 4 red A (8 total A); 4 black-and-red B

Bias stems: 4 green, 4½ each; 4 green, 11" each (62" total)

Straight stems: 1 bluish green, 8½"; 1 burgundy, 8½" (17" total)

BLOCK 48

Designed by Jo Moury,
Haymarket, Virginia, United States

Cutting

Blossoms: 4 blue A, 4 red B

Leaves: 8 bluish green A, 8 dark green B

Circles: 4 dark gold A, 4 orange A, 4 red A,
4 black-and-red A, 4 gold A, 8 green-and-
yellow A, 12 pinkish brown A (40 total A)

Bias stems: 4 green, 2½" each; 4 green, 10" each
(50" total)

BLOCK 49

Designed by Elizabeth Phillips,
Rapid City, South Dakota, United States

Cutting

Blossoms: 6 red C, 2 orange C (8 total C)

Leaves: 9 green B, 7 dark green B, 4 bluish
green B (20 total B)

Circles: 6 burgundy A, 2 black-and-red A
(8 total A)

Bias stems: 4 green, 9" each (36" total)

BLOCK 50

Designed by Joan Lucchese,
Walnut Creek, California, United States

Cutting

Blossoms: 4 bluish green A, 8 light green B, 8 red D

Leaves: 4 light green B, 4 bluish green D

Circles: 8 red A, 4 light green B

Bias stems: 4 burgundy, 4" each; 4 burgundy, 5" each (36" total)

BLOCK 51

Designed by Dorothy Richey,
Dunwoody, Georgia, United States

Blossoms: 5 red C, 5 orange D, 5 red E, 1 orange F, 1 red G

Leaves: 16 green A

Circles: 5 gold B, 5 red C, 5 orange D

Bias stems: 4 green, 4" each (16" total)

BLOCK 52

*Designed by Dorothy Richey,
Dunwoody, Georgia, United States*

Cutting

Blossoms: 1 red C, 4 orange C (5 total C);
1 orange D, 4 red D (5 total D); 1 red E,
4 orange E (5 total E); 1 orange F, 4 gold F
(5 total F); 1 gold G

Leaves: 4 green B

Circles: 5 gold B; 4 orange C; 1 orange D,
4 red D (5 total D)

Bias stems: 8 green, 5" each (40" total)

BLOCK 53

*Designed by Dorothy Richey,
Dunwoody, Georgia, United States*

Cutting

Blossoms: 1 gold A, 8 red B, 4 red C, 1 red D,
1 red E

Leaves: 32 dark green A

Circles: 4 gold A; 4 gold B; 4 orange B (8 total
B); 8 orange C; 4 red D

Bias stems: 4 dark green, 6" each (24" total)

Straight stems: 4 dark green, 4" each (16" total)

BLOCK 54

Designed by Michelle Ann Fairchild,
Crosby, Minnesota, United States

Cutting

Blossoms: 1 dark gold A, 1 gold A, 2 green-
and-yellow A, 1 red A, 1 orange A (6 total
A); 1 pinkish brown B, 3 orange B (4 total
B); 1 gold C, 1 green-and-yellow C,
2 black-and-red C (4 total C); 2 red E

Leaves: 1 light green A, 2 bluish green A
(3 total A); 2 green B, 2 dark green B,
5 bluish green B (9 total B); 1 green C,
1 light green C, 2 bluish green C, 2 red C
(6 total C); 1 dark green D; 1 dark green E

Circles: 2 gold A

Straight stems: 12 assorted colors (4 burgundy,
4 blue, 4 pinkish brown), 12½" each
(150" total)

BLOCK 55

Designed by Michelle Ann Fairchild,
Crosby, Minnesota, United States

Cutting

Blossoms: 2 black-and-red A; 2 blue B; 4 gold
D; 2 pinkish brown E; 2 red F, 2 blue F
(4 total F); 2 red G

Leaves: 4 green B, 4 blue C

Circles: 2 black-and-red C

Bias stems: 2 pinkish brown, 8" each;
2 burgundy, 8" each (32" total)

BLOCK 56

*Designed by Jacquelyn Jacobi,
Victoria, British Columbia, Canada*

Cutting

Blossoms: 4 black-and-red B, 4 dark gold D

Leaves: 8 red A, 8 light green A, 16 blue A (32 total A); 8 light green B

Circles: 4 orange A

Bias stems: 4 green, 9" each (36" total)

Straight stems: 4 green, 3" each (12" total)

BLOCK 57

*Designed by Jacquelyn Jacobi,
Victoria, British Columbia, Canada*

Cutting

Blossoms: 5 blue B

Leaves: 10 gold A; 5 bluish green D, 10 red D (15 total D)

Circles: 5 dark gold C

Bias stems: 5 green, 2½" each (12½" total)

BLOCK 58

*Designed by Jacquelyn Jacobi,
Victoria, British Columbia, Canada*

Cutting

Blossoms: 6 red B

Leaves: 2 green A, 1 blue A (3 total A); 1 dark green B, 1 bluish green B (2 total B); 1 green C; 3 green D, 2 light green D, 1 bluish green D (6 total D)

Circles: 6 dark gold A, 1 gold D

Stems: 2 green, 1" each; 1 green, 1¾" (3¾" total bias or straight grain)

BLOCK 59

*Designed by Jacquelyn Jacobi,
Victoria, British Columbia, Canada*

Cutting

Blossoms: 4 black-and-red C

Leaves: 4 gold F, 4 red F, 4 green F, 4 blue F (16 total F)

Circles: 4 dark gold B

BLOCK 60

Designed by Barb Vlack,
Saint Charles, Illinois, United States

Blossoms: 1 orange C, 1 red E

Leaves: 8 bluish green B, 4 blue C,
    4 dark green E

Circles: 61 assorted colors B

Straight stems: 4 dark green, 3" each (12" total)

BLOCK 61

Designed by Judy Messenger,
Toronto, Ontario, Canada

Cutting

Blossoms: none

Leaves: 1 bluish green A, 6 orange A (7 total
    A); 2 light green B; 1 green C, 8 red C
    (9 total C); 3 green D; 2 green F

Circles: 6 gold A, 8 bluish green A (14 total A);
    8 dark gold B, 3 red B, 3 black-and-red B
    (14 total B); 1 green-and-yellow C,
    8 blue C (9 total C); 2 gold D, 2 green D,
    2 pinkish brown D (6 total D)

Bias stems (left to right): 1 dark green, 1½";
    1 dark green, 6"; 1 dark green, 5½"; 1 dark
    green, 8½"; 1 dark green, 4½"; 1 dark
    green, 2"; 1 dark green, 7"; 1 dark green, 5";
    1 dark green, 2" (42" total)

BLOCK 62

Designed by Judy Best,
London, Ontario, Canada

Cutting

Blossoms: 2 blue B, 2 light green B (4 total B); 2 gold C, 2 orange C, 2 blue C, 2 bluish green C (8 total C); 2 burgundy E, 2 red E, (4 total E)

Leaves: 1 dark gold B, 1 pinkish brown B, 2 red B, 8 green B, 4 dark green B, 4 bluish green B (20 total B)

Circles: 2 gold B, 2 green-and-yellow B (4 total B); 2 black-and-red C, 2 green-and-yellow C (4 total C)

Bias stems: 4 dark green, 3" each; 8 dark green, 3¼" each (38" total)

BLOCK 63

Designed by Carolyn Laukkonen,
Richmond, British Columbia, Canada

Cutting

Blossoms: 1 red A, 1 black-and-red A, 1 burgundy A (3 total A); 1 gold C; 1 orange D; 1 bluish green F; 1 orange J; 1 bluish green L

Leaves: 2 bluish green D; 2 green F

Circles: 2 background A, 3 gold A (5 total A); 1 background D, 1 pinkish brown D (2 total D)

BLOCK 64

*Designed by Carolyn Laukkonen,
Richmond, British Columbia, Canada*

Cutting

Blossoms: 3 pinkish brown A, 4 red A (7 total
A); 1 orange B, 2 gold B (3 total B); 1 gold
C, 2 orange C (3 total C)

Leaves: 3 bluish green B; 1 bluish green D,
2 pinkish brown D, 3 background D
(6 total D); 3 pinkish brown F

Circles: 1 burgundy A, 3 bluish green A,
3 blue A, 6 gold A (13 total A);
3 burgundy B; 3 burgundy C

BLOCK 65

*Designed by Carolyn Laukkonen,
Richmond, British Columbia, Canada*

Cutting

Blossoms: 4 burgundy A, 4 red B, 4 gold C

Leaves: 4 light green B; 4 bluish green D; 4
green E, 4 bluish green E, 4 light green E
(12 total E)

Circles: 4 red A, 4 gold B, 4 burgundy C

BLOCK 66

*Designed by Carolyn Laukkonen,
Richmond, British Columbia, Canada*

Cutting

Blossoms: 2 red A, 8 gold A (10 total A);
1 red B, 4 gold B (5 total B); 9 red C

Leaves: 6 light green A, 6 bluish green A
(12 total A); 6 pinkish brown B

Circles: 13 orange A, 15 burgundy A (28 total
A); 9 burgundy B

BLOCK 67

*Designed by Christiane Wipplinger,
Ruesselsheim, Germany*

Cutting

Blossoms: 1 orange D, 8 red D, (9 total D);
1 red F

Leaves: 16 green A

Circles: 1 gold D, 8 orange D (9 total D)

Bias stems: 4 pinkish brown, 13½" each
(54" total)

BLOCK 68

Designed by Norma Evans,
Oxford, Alabama, United States

Cutting

Blossoms: 4 gold A, 6 dark gold A (10 total A); 1 black-and-red D, 4 burgundy D (5 total D)

Leaves: 4 green A, 8 dark gold A (12 total A)

Bias stems: 10 black-and-red, 3" each; 4 black-and-red, 5½" each (52" total)

BLOCK 69

Designed by Carol Campbell,
Drogheda, County Meath, Ireland

Cutting

Blossoms: 1 gold C, 1 burgundy C, 2 blue C (4 total C); 1 red E; 1 orange F, 1 black-and-red F, 1 burgundy F (3 total F); 1 red I

Leaves: 5 green A, 3 green B, 3 green C

Circles: 1 orange A; 2 pinkish brown B, 1 orange B, 1 red B (4 total B); 2 gold C; 1 gold D

Bias stems: 1 green, 4¼"; 1 green, 6¼"; 1 green, 8½"; 1 burgundy, 7¼" (26¼" total)

BLOCK 70

Designed by Carol Campbell,
Drogheda, County Meath, Ireland

Cutting

Blossoms: 1 burgundy A, 2 orange A (3 total A); 1 orange B, 2 gold B, 3 red B (6 total B); 2 orange D; 6 black-and-red K

Leaves: 6 orange A, 6 burgundy A, 7 green A (19 total A); 3 green B; 6 red C; 6 burgundy D; 6 dark gold E

Circles: 1 red A; 1 orange B, 1 gold B 1 dark gold B (3 total B)

Bias stems: 2 green, 2" each; 2 green, 4½" each; 1 green, 5½"; 1 green, 9½" (28" total)

BLOCK 71

Designed by Jennifer Hope,
Fort Wayne, Indiana, United States

Cutting

Blossoms: 4 black-and-red F

Leaves: 16 blue A, 4 bluish green C

Circles: 4 orange A, 4 light green A (8 total A); 4 light green B; 4 light green D

Bias stems: 2 green, 9" each (18" total)

60

BLOCK 72

Designed by Judy Messenger,
Toronto, Ontario, Canada

Cutting

Blossoms: 4 gold C, 1 dark gold G, 1 burgundy H, 1 green-and-yellow J

Leaves: 2 orange A, 2 bluish green A, 2 light green A, 4 blue A, 6 red A, 8 pinkish brown A (24 total A); 2 orange B, 2 bluish green B, 2 light green B, 4 blue B, 6 red B (16 total B)

Circles: 8 pinkish brown A, 4 green B, 4 burgundy C, 1 dark green D

BLOCK 73

Designed by Kari Bauer,
Oak Park, Illinois, United States

Cutting

Blossoms: 1 red C, 1 gold E, 1 orange G, 1 red I

Leaves: 2 bluish green C, 2 light green D, 2 blue E, 1 blue F

Circles: 1 gold A, 2 green A, 4 green-and-yellow A (7 total A); 1 orange B, 2 green B, 4 dark gold B (7 total B); 1 red C, 1 black-and-red C, 1 green C, 4 pinkish brown C (7 total C); 1 red D, 2 burgundy D (3 total D)

Bias stems: 2 light green, 11" each; 2 bluish green, 25" each (72" total)

BLOCK 74

*Designed by Kari Bauer,
Oak Park, Illinois, United States*

Cutting

Blossoms: 1 red C, 1 orange E, 1 gold G,
1 red I

Leaves: 4 light green D; 4 green E, 4 blue E
(8 total E); 2 bluish green F, 2 green F
(4 total F)

Circles: 4 green-and-yellow B; 1 black-and-red
C, 4 dark gold C (5 total C)

Bias stems: 4 dark green, 15" each (60" total)

BLOCK 75

*Designed by Kari Bauer,
Oak Park, Illinois, United States*

Cutting

Blossoms: 4 red A, 4 orange B, 4 gold C,
4 orange D, 4 red E

Leaves: 8 light green A, 8 blue B, 4 blue C

Circles: 4 black-and-red A

Bias stems: 8 gold, 9½" each (76" total)

Straight stems: 4 dark green, 3½" each
(14" total)

BLOCK 76

Designed by Claudia Chang,
Taipei, Taiwan

Cutting

Blossoms: 4 red F, 4 blue D, 1 red D (5 total D)

Leaves: 32 blue A

Circles: 48 pinkish brown A, 16 gold A,
4 burgundy A (68 total A); 5 gold C

BLOCK 77

Designed by Pat Daniels,
Winnipeg, Manitoba, Canada

Cutting

Blossoms: 2 gold A; 1 orange B, 2 bluish green
B (3 total B); 1 orange C, 1 blue C, 1 red C
(3 total C); 2 dark gold D, 2 blue D (4 total
D); 2 blue E

Leaves: 5 dark green A, 6 bluish green A (11
total A); 4 green B, 4 light green B (8 total
B); 1 green C, 1 dark green C, 2 light green
C (4 total C); 4 green D

Circles: 2 black-and-red A, 1 red B, 2 green-
and-yellow C, 2 red D

Straight stems: 1 pinkish brown, 6½";
1 pinkish brown, 5¼"; 1 pinkish brown, 5";
2 pinkish brown, 4" each; 1 pinkish brown,
3½"; 1 pinkish brown, 2" (30¼" total)

BLOCK 78

Designed by Lida Letey,
Delta, Colorado, United States

Cutting

Blossoms: none

Leaves: 10 bluish green C, 10 burgundy F

Circles: 1 green-and-yellow A; 10 green-and-
   yellow B; 1 bluish green C, 10 red C (11
   total C); 1 red D

BLOCK 79

Designed by Dorothy Richey,
Dunwoody, Georgia, United States

Cutting

Blossoms: 10 red B, 1 orange C

Leaves: 35 light green A, 5 pinkish-brown C

Circles: 1 gold A, 1 dark gold B, 10 dark gold
   C, 1 red D

Bias stems: 5 green, 2" each; 5 green, 2½" each
   (22½" total)

BLOCK 80

Designed by Joan Lucchese,
Walnut Creek, California, United States

Cutting

Blossoms: 6 red A, 3 green A (9 total A); 3 orange B, 3 bluish green B, 3 pinkish brown B (9 total B); 6 blue C, 3 bluish green C (9 total C)

Leaves: 7 green A

Circles: 3 green-and-yellow A, 3 orange A, 3 red A, 9 dark gold A (18 total A)

Straight stems: 2 bluish green, 3" each; 1 bluish green, 2¼" (8¼" total)

BLOCK 81

Designed by Kerri Elizabeth Edwards,
Riva, Maryland, United States

Cutting

Blossoms: 1 red D, 1 orange E, 1 red G, 1 red I

Leaves: 28 green B

Circles: 1 gold B; 4 orange D, 4 red D (8 total D)

Bias stems: 8 burgundy, 2½" each (20" total)

BLOCK 82

Designed by Christiane Wipplinger,
Ruesselsheim, Germany

Cutting

Blossoms: 8 burgundy A, 8 red C

Leaves: 8 blue A, 16 blue B

Bias stems: 4 bluish green, 16" each (32" total)

BLOCK 83

Designed by Anneke de Weerdt,
Rotterdam, Netherlands

Cutting

Blossoms: 1 gold B, 1 orange D, 1 red F

Leaves: 8 light green D, 8 dark green E

Circles: 8 orange A, 8 orange C

Machine-Embroidered Wall Hanging

Finished size: 10" x 28"

I have a small space in my studio that has always cried out for something pretty, but as it's very narrow, I've never managed to find anything that I thought was the right proportion. So, when we received the appliquéd and machine-embroidered Rose of Sharon blocks from Oklahoma Embroidery Supply and Design (see page 91), I knew I'd found what I needed. I just love seeing the smaller versions of blocks I've made in the 12" size. You might recognize the bottom block. It's Block 4, but the other two were designed before the block challenge took place, so they're not included in the gallery. They are, however, all included in the OESD CD. If you want to appliqué your blocks, you have 83 to choose from! For templates, reduce the patterns on page 90 to 58%.

MATERIALS

⅜ yard of off-white fabric for background

⅜ yard of fabric for backing

¼ yard of fabric for binding

3 pieces of batting 12" x 12"

Assorted scraps for blossoms

Assorted threads for embroidery

2 yards of grosgrain ribbon for hanging tabs
    and mounting strips*

Hanging rod

Freezer paper

Compass

If you can't find ribbon that matches your project, buy ⅜ yard of binding fabric and create hanging tabs and mounting strips from that.

CUTTING

From the fabric for background, cut:

3 squares, 12" x 12", or whatever size is required to fit the hoop on your embroidery machine

From the fabric for backing, cut:

3 squares, 12" x 12"

From the fabric for binding, cut:

3 strips, 2" x 42"

1 strip, 2" x 42", if making your own hanging tabs and mounting strips

CREATING THE HEXAGONS

1. Cut two 12" squares of freezer paper and iron them shiny sides together.

2. Find the center of the square and draw a circle with a radius of 5" inches.

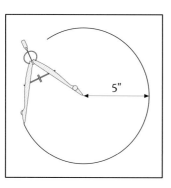

3. Without changing the compass width, move the point of the compass to a point on the circle directly left of the center.

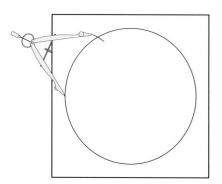

4. Mark the circle, move the compass point to that mark, and mark the circle again. Connect the two marks to make the first side of your hexagon.

Machine-Embroidered Rose of Sharon

I know all of you have been impressed by the incredibly beautiful things being done on embroidery machines, and we were delighted when Oklahoma Embroidery Supply and Design (OESD) digitized both the winning blocks and some of our earlier designs. Being able to both appliqué and embroider on these amazing machines opens up many new doors for quilters.

OESD has produced a Rose of Sharon Block CD, which includes all of the winning blocks plus 18 others from the Challenge. See "Resources" on page 91. The 12 winning blocks are approximately 9½" square and the 18 additional blocks are approximately 5" square. Follow your machine manufacturer's instructions for best results.

5. Continue to mark around the circle and connect the marks until you have six sides. Create a window template by cutting on the lines of the hexagon.

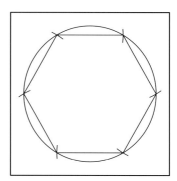

6. Center your template on the background square and, with a washable marker, mark the hexagon shape on your background, making sure a flat side of the hexagon is parallel to the top of the square.

7. If using the OESD Rose of Sharon Block CD, follow your sewing-machine manufacturer's instructions, and embroider your three chosen designs. If you choose to appliqué the blocks, reduce the size of the patterns on page 90 by 58% for your templates. For full-size placement diagrams, enlarge the photos of blocks 1–13 by 116%, and blocks 14–83 by 175%. Whichever method you use, make sure the designs are centered in the middle of the hexagons.

8. Layer and quilt as desired. Trim around each block, leaving ¼" beyond the drawn hexagon lines.

Trim ¼" beyond drawn line.

9. Bind each of the three blocks. I used a 2"-wide strip to achieve the narrow binding. As the corners are 120°, not 90°, I recommend you use the Binding Miter Tool from Animas Quilts to get the right angle on your miters. (See "Resources" on page 91.)

Joining the Three Blocks

I was unable to find the perfect ribbon to join my blocks, so I made strips using the same fabric as my binding.

1. If you're using ribbon for the hanging tabs and mounting strips, skip to step 2. If making your own hanging strips, cut a strip 2" x 42". Fold lengthwise with wrong sides together and sew using a ⅛" seam allowance. Centering the seam allowance on the back, press the strip. This produces a ¾"-wide strip that's finished on one side. When joining the blocks, just make sure you have the "pretty" side facing the front.

2. On each of two pieces of grosgrain ribbon or your hanging strips, fold back enough ribbon to accommodate whatever hanging rod you've chosen.

3. Position each ribbon so that the loops formed extend above the binding on the top blocks. Insert a hanging rod in the top loops and pin in place. If your hanging rod has an enclosed end, you must insert it before sewing the loops down.

4. Pin each ribbon in a straight line to the bottom of the first block, and from the right side stitch in the ditch formed by the binding, attaching the ribbon to the top and the bottom of the block.

5. Leaving ¾" of ribbon between the two blocks, pin the middle block at both the top and the bottom edges. Again, stitch in the ditch.

6. Leaving ¾" of ribbon between the two blocks, pin the bottom block at the top edge. Trim the ribbon, leaving enough to hem the bottom before sewing the final block on. Sew the hem.

7. Stitch in the ditch at the top of the final block.

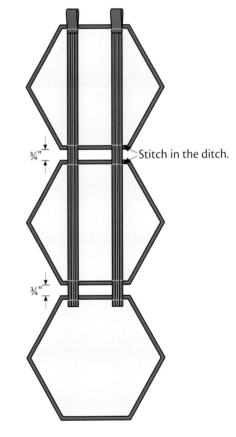

You now have a lovely wall hanging for yourself or a lucky friend.

Machine-Embroidered Pillow

Finished size: 18" x 18"

I'm a big fan of throw pillows. You can do so much with them, and they're so easy to make—even easier if you have an embroidery module on your machine. My favorite type is the flange pillow. The flange—essentially a border—gives a small pillow more substance, and it gives you more space to do some quilting if you want. After working with 12" finished blocks for what seems like months (happy months, I want you to know), I really wanted to see what sort of secondary pattern I'd get if I combined four 6" blocks. So, I chose a favorite block that we designed before the Quilt Challenge took place. It isn't included in the Block Gallery but it is on the Oklahoma Embroidery Supply and Design CD (see page 91). If you want to appliqué 6" blocks, use the photograph for blocks 1–13 as a full-size placement guide, or enlarge the pattern for blocks 14–83 150%. Or you may prefer to appliqué a 12" block for your pillow.

MATERIALS

4 squares, 8" x 8", or a 14" x 14" piece of background fabric (follow your sewing-machine manufacturer's instructions for the size of background square you need to embroider a 6" or 12" finished block)

¼ yard of fabric for border (not a fat quarter)

½ yard of fabric for backing

18" x 18" piece batting

18" x 18" piece muslin

Assorted scraps for blossoms

Assorted threads for embroidery

Fiberfill to stuff your pillow

11" of Velcro or 3 buttons for closing

CUTTING

From the border fabric, cut:
- 2 strips, 3½" x 12½"
- 2 strips, 3½" x 18½"

From the backing fabric, cut:
- 2 rectangles, 18½" x 13¼"

MAKING THE TOP

1. Embroider or appliqué four designs, 6" x 6" each, in the middle of the four 8" background squares. To appliqué 6" blocks, reduce the patterns on page 90 by 50% for your templates. For full-size placement diagrams, use the photographs for blocks 1–13 or enlarge the patterns for blocks 14–83 by 150%. Trim each embroidered or appliquéd square to 6½". Sew the four squares together as for a Four Patch block.

   For one 12" block, embroider or appliqué the design in the middle of a 14" background square. Trim the square to 12½". Always follow the sewing-machine manufacturer's instructions when embroidering the blocks.

2. Sew the two 3½" x 12½" border strips to the sides of the 12½" square. Press the seam allowances toward the border.

3. Sew the two 3½" x 18½" border strips to the top and bottom of the square. Press the seam allowances toward the border.

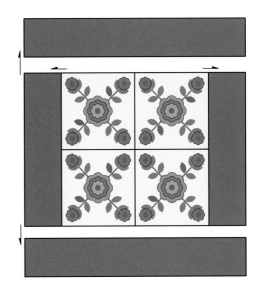

LAYERING AND QUILTING

1. Center an 18" square of batting and an 18" square of muslin on the wrong side of the 18½" pillow top. We do not want batting and muslin to extend to the edge of the top, as we will be "pillow slipping" the top together, and we don't want batting in the seam.

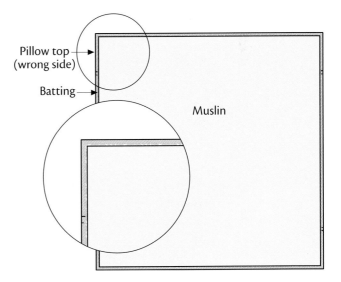

2. Quilt as desired.

ASSEMBLY AND FINISHING

1. On each of the two backing pieces, turn under 1½" on the 18½" side and press; turn under 1½" one more time and stitch close to the edge to hem.

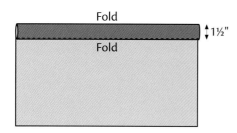

2. Apply pieces of Velcro along the hem underneath one backing piece and on the top of the other, making sure they line up and that when they overlap they will make an 18½" square. Or, make buttonholes on one hem and sew buttons on the other. Keep the Velcro or the buttons 4" from the top and bottom or they will interfere with the flange.

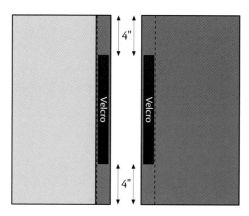

3. Line up the Velcro pieces, or button the two pieces together and baste along the top and bottom, inside the ¼" seam allowance.

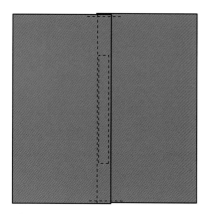

Align Velcro and baste pieces together.

4. With right sides together and using a ¼" seam allowance, sew the back and front of the pillow together. By opening either the Velcro or buttons, turn the pillow right side out and press the seam flat.

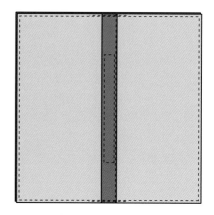

5. Topstitch around the pillow ¼" from the edge.

6. With invisible thread, stitch in the ditch around the center square.

Topstitch ¼"   Stitch in
from edge.   the ditch.

7. Undo the buttons or Velcro closing and insert enough fiberfill to fluff the pillow up to your liking. Or, you can make a small pillow form and fill it with fiberfill.

For Inspiration

Roses of Recollection

Finished size: 50" x 61"

When my dear friend Margaret Miller heard about the Rose of Sharon Block Challenge, she phoned and offered to "do anything" to help further the project along. Of course, I immediately suggested that she come and clean my house, thereby freeing me to do some more appliqué. Then reality set in, and I realized how selfish that would be. What we really wanted from Margaret was to have her do her magic and give you another way to put your Rose of Sharon blocks together.

What a combination: beautifully embroidered and appliquéd blocks by Oklahoma Embroidery Supply and Design put into a show-stopping quilt by Margaret J. Miller, quilted by Wanda Rains.

Roses Revisited

Finished size: 58¾" x 58¾"

When I opened the box from Oklahoma Embroidery Supply and Design with the appliquéd and embroidered blocks in it, I couldn't believe my eyes. Up to that point I had seen only machine-embroidered work, not the wonderful appliquéd and embroidered work that you see here. Isn't technology wonderful? Now we can combine appliqué and embroidery for even more beautiful results.

I used a slightly different setting for these great blocks, and this quilt was put together the conventional way so it could be quilted on a long-arm quilting machine by Wanda Rains. Additional quilting was done by Coreen Zerr. The finished block size is 11"; the faux piping does not increase the size of the block or the border. The sashing is 1" wide finished and the border is 3" wide finished.

Invisible Machine Appliqué

My favorite method of appliqué is invisible machine appliqué, which succeeds in appliquéing the pieces with as little of the thread showing as possible. Sometimes the edges are turned under and sometimes the appliqué piece is fused, but in both cases I try to make the thread invisible.

You'll notice the word "machine" used in that description, and here I must tell you that I'm a hardcore machine quiltmaker. It's not that I don't appreciate hand work, it's just that I don't have time to do it. But, I will assure all of you hand-appliqué fans out there that you can follow the directions for my type of appliqué up to the point where the fabric is to be stitched, and then you can just ignore all the instructions about what machine needle and thread to use. You obviously know which hand-sewing needles and threads you like—or you wouldn't be a dedicated hand appliquér—so you can just find your favorite chair and sit yourself down to do some hand work. The rest of you will have to go through the machine instructions first. Or, maybe not. You might already have your own technique figured out, in which case you also can ignore my suggestions and just get on with your own method.

As you can see, I'm not the kind of instructor who insists on "my way"—whatever way works for you is the best way, and don't let anybody tell you differently.

Now that we have that out of the way, let's get on to how I do invisible machine appliqué.

The Tools You Need to Do the Job

I advise all of my classes to buy only good-quality tools—you deserve them! For machine appliqué, you'll need all the standard machine-quilting tools, plus a few specific items covered in this section.

Needles

For appliqué by machine that is truly invisible we'll be using the smallest needle we can find, which is a 60/8. The next thing to look for would be a machine needle that doesn't leave permanent holes in the fabric, because that's often the clue that gives away that a piece has been done by machine. Not that it's anything to be ashamed of.

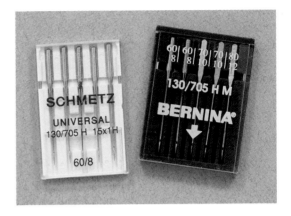

Size 60/8 is my favorite size for invisible machine appliqué.

If your goal is to create something that doesn't show a row of machine-created holes, what better needle to use than one that doesn't pierce a fiber—my favorite—the underappreciated Universal needle.

The Universal needle was designed for the domestic sewer who often had to switch between knit and woven fabrics. When knits were first introduced to the domestic sewing market, it was necessary to switch from the Sharp needles we'd been using to one with a more rounded tip, a ball-point, or stretch, needle. But, what happened was that we often forgot which needle we had in the machine, and if a Sharp needle was used to sew knits it would pierce a fiber and cause a run in the fabric. This did not make us happy, I can tell you. So, the manufacturers of domestic sewing-machine needles took pity on us and created a needle that could be used interchangeably. It's not as sharp as the Sharp needles, nor as rounded as ball-point needles, and it can be used on both knits and wovens with good results.

Now it's the perfect needle to use for invisible machine appliqué, and it does a good job of sewing seams, but it's a poor choice for any type of surface design. If the thread is going to be visible you should not use a Universal needle, as it will produce random little zigzag stitches. The reason of course is because it won't pierce a fiber; if it hits one it's diverted to one side or the other. So, what makes it perfect for invisible machine appliqué makes it a bad choice for any surface design where the thread will be visible.

Thread

Continuing with our search for the best way to make our machine appliqué truly invisible we'll try to find the perfect thread to go with our ultra-fine needles. My first choice for thread is always cotton, and if I can find the perfect color to match my appliqué, that's what I will go for always. The problem is that often the fabric I'm using is multicolored or many values of the same color; either way it's impossible to find one thread that will match all of those variables.

Let's assume, though, that sometimes you *will* be using fabric with just one color for your appliqué and you've found the perfect-colored thread. So, what weight should you use? In cotton (if the English numbering system is used) the finest thread is 60/2—although the numbers aren't always on the spool. Some companies refer to their finest threads (I'm referring here to size not quality) as embroidery thread, so if you can find the right color and the right weight, I recommend cotton.

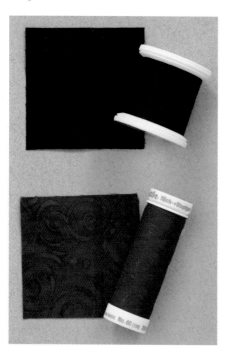

See how the thread just disappears against the fabric.

So that leaves us with the problem of what to use when our appliqué fabric is multicolored. The solution, I think, is to use invisible monofilament thread, which comes in two decorator colors, smoke and clear. I'm not partial to a particular fiber content in invisible threads; I've had good results with both invisible polyester and nylon. What I do look for is a fine-enough invisible thread, one that won't damage the cotton fabric I'm using.

The size I look for is .004, but if there is no size printed on the spool, I do the "break test." After you buy the thread, unwind a piece and try to break it. If you end up with rope burns on your finger, it's too strong, and it will damage your fabric. If, however, it breaks easily, it's fine enough to use.

When using monofilament, I always test both smoke and clear to see which one is least visible against my fabric.

My all-time favorite bobbin thread, when doing invisible machine appliqué, is 50/3 medium-gray cotton. I've had great success with it, and, because it's the thread I use to sew my blocks together, I always have it on hand.

Medium-gray cotton thread is my first choice to use in the bobbin.

Freezer Paper

I couldn't get through one day of quilting without my freezer paper. You can purchase it at the grocery store, and I always have some on hand. All of the drawing is done on the dull side, and when you iron the shiny side to your fabric, it sticks. For this technique we'll be ironing it to the wrong side of our fabric, but I know some hand appliquérs iron it to the right side and use it to do needle-turned edges (a complete mystery to me as the dedicated machine person that I am). If freezer paper peels off before you're ready to use the fabric piece, you can just touch it again with the iron to re-stick it. It leaves no residue on your fabric, and if the template isn't damaged when you remove it, you can use it again.

For those of you who hate cutting out templates, you'll be delighted to learn that precut Rose of Sharon freezer-paper templates are available from the Nine Patch Media website (see "Resources" on page 91), and if you're a lucky owner of one of the AccuQuilt Cutting machines, there's a Rose of Sharon die for both the Studio and GO! machines that will cut out both templates and fabric.

Imagine how many Rose of Sharon blocks you could cut with one of these in your studio!

But for you DIY types, all you have to do is trace the patterns provided onto the dull side of freezer paper using *pencil* only. The reason is that one of my favorite glues to hold things in place is rubber cement, and the combination of ink and rubber cement is ugly. Picture gloppy stuff all over your lovely appliqué fabric.

Adhesives

I use adhesives for two things—tacking the seam allowance onto templates and positioning pieces, especially stems.

I've found the best way to keep the seam allowance turned onto your templates is to glue it, and the material that works best for me is rubber cement. It comes from the hardware store, and on your way home from the hardware store, you can stop at the dollar store and buy some cheap disposable bristle brushes. My dollar store sells them for about 10 cents a piece, but when you get them home, you'll have to give them a haircut. They're designed

for painting, and I find that with the bristles as long as they are, it's hard to control where the glue goes.

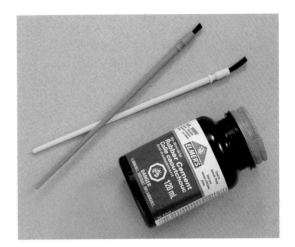

Give your disposable brushes a haircut by trimming the bristles.

Rubber cement sticks only to itself, so it's necessary to put some on the freezer paper and some on the fabric. As soon as it dries (it will no longer be shiny when it dries), you can roll the seam allowance over onto the freezer paper and it will hold for years and years. It will also let go when you want it to. If you've found a pucker or pleat on the edge of your appliqué piece, you can just peel it back and reposition it. That ability to let go is even more important when you want to remove the freezer paper after you've stitched the appliqué piece in place. The downside to rubber cement is the odor. It's absolutely necessary to work in a well-ventilated area when using it.

Another option—one that doesn't smell as bad—is a *repositionable* glue stick. One is put out by SewLine (also marketed with the name Fons and Porter), and Scotch brand has one as well. Glue sticks have some drawbacks; the smaller ones get used up pretty quickly, and the larger ones are hard to control. I find when working on small pieces it's hard to get the glue only where I want it.

Repositionable glue sticks can be used instead of rubber cement.

I recently discovered Liquid Stitch, and I am in love. It is the absolute best thing to hold your bias (and straight-grain) stems in place until you get them stitched down. It's a permanent, clear drying, nontoxic adhesive, which comes in a plastic bottle with an applicator tip. I squeeze a small bead of Liquid Stitch on the background fabric where my stems are to go, and then gently press the stems onto the glue. It holds them exactly where I want them and they don't get distorted when going under the presser foot on your machine.

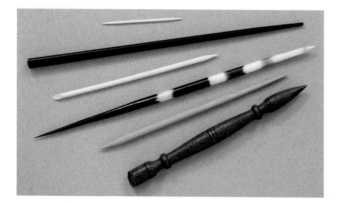

Liquid Stitch is perfect for holding stems in place.

Turning Tools

To turn the seam allowance over onto the edge of the freezer-paper template, you'll want to use a tool that is comfortable to work with—and if you're like me you'll also want it to be beautiful. I love it when I can find a tool that's not just functional, but also something that I love to look at and hold in my hand. Before I found my lovely hand-tooled appliqué stylus, I worked my way through many other tools, which are pictured below.

From the top we have the lowly round toothpick, a chopstick, an orange stick (from the manicure department at the drugstore), a porcupine quill, a bamboo stylus, and finally my favorite hand-tooled appliqué stylus.

Sewing-Machine Foot

My favorite foot for invisible machine appliqué is the open-toed embroidery foot, which gives you an unobstructed view of the needle. If you're a Bernina owner, it's the number 20 foot. If your machine doesn't have a similar foot, look for the one that gives you the best visibility—and do consider modifying a foot if necessary. The pieces of metal or plastic that cross in front of the needle can often be ground off without any loss of function—and of course for our purposes it improves them greatly. If you have one, get out your Dremel hand-held rotary tool and grind off the bits you don't want.

A good foot provides maximum visibility for stitching.

THE PERFECT STITCH

I often see machine-appliquéd quilts that are very appealing until I get up close, and then I'm distracted by the amount of thread that is visible. Now, if you've made a conscious decision to make the thread part of the design, that's fine. But if your intention was to make it invisible, then a blanket stitch or even the blind hem stitch aren't great choices. What you need is a stitch that is strong yet unobtrusive, and the homely little zigzag stitch fills the bill.

When you set your machine to do a zigzag stitch, the default width is too wide and the length is too close together. I think the manufacturers assume we're going to make a buttonhole when we choose that stitch—silly people.

Choose the zigzag stitch, and then adjust the width all the way down to .5. Or if your machine uses a different system of sizing, just set it to the narrowest width you can while still being able to see the needle moving from left to right. Next, we want the stitch to be longer than the default, and my choice is 2.5 for length. If your machine uses a different numbering system, you're aiming for a stitch that looks like this (stitches are shown exact size).

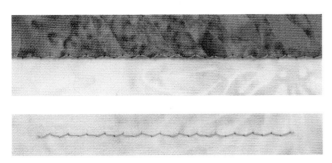

A narrow zigzag stitch will almost disappear when the right thread is used. Can you see the stitches joining the green fabric to the white piece? The same-size stitch was used to create the visible row of green stitches.

It is barely off a straight stitch, but if the needle, when going to the right, is in the background fabric, and when going to the left just catches the very edge of your appliqué fabric, then your stitch will be almost invisible. That's assuming you have those itty-bitty needles and some super-fine cotton thread or invisible nylon or polyester in the machine.

Now that we have all of the tools we need, it's time to jump right in and do some machine appliqué.

Edge-Turned Invisible Machine Appliqué

Step-by-step, here's how I do it:

1. Choose one of the blossom shapes on page 90 and trace it onto the dull side of freezer paper using pencil only. You can staple up to 4 layers of paper together if you need multiple copies of the same-size blossom. Be sure to put the one with your drawing on it on top.

2. Cut on the drawn line—do *not* add a seam allowance. If you've layered the freezer paper, remove the staples. I find it best to keep the same-size templates in a baggie.

3. Iron the shiny side of the freezer paper to the wrong side of your appliqué fabric.

4. Trim around the edge of the freezer paper, leaving between ⅛" and ¼" for the seam allowance, and then clip the inside corners.

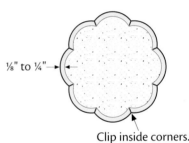

⅛" to ¼"

Clip inside corners.

5. Apply a little bit of rubber cement to both the freezer paper and the fabric—you'll quickly learn how much is enough—and when it's dry, turn the seam allowance over onto the freezer paper. I also find it helpful to mark the starting point when I'm gluing. When the glue is dry, it's almost invisible, and if you're interrupted while gluing, you might not be able to see where you left off. Add a dab of Fray Check to each of the inside corners where you clipped the seam. The clipped corners are weak spots and the Fray Check will strengthen them.

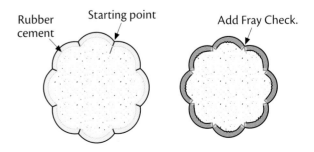

Rubber cement   Starting point   Add Fray Check.

6. To make it easier to keep everything in the right place, tape a placement guide to a light box, and then line up your background fabric on top of it. Position the appliqué piece onto the background fabric using the placement guide and tape it in place. I use transparent (not masking) tape instead of pins, particularly when working with small pieces, as the motion of putting a pin through the freezer paper almost always shifts the piece.

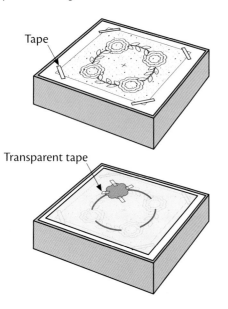

Tape

Transparent tape

7. Set up your machine with the appropriate thread, needle, and foot. Start by anchoring your stitches with about ¼" of tiny straight stitches right up against the edge of the appliqué piece—but stitch only into the background fabric. Then change to your very narrow zigzag stitch and sew around the piece, pivoting whenever necessary. Remember, when the needle is to the right, it should be in the background fabric, and when it's to the left, it should be catching just the very edge of the appliqué. At the end change back to the straight stitch and, again with tiny stitches, anchor the end of the stitching into the background fabric only.

Straight stitches

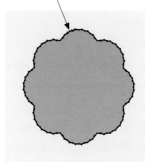

8. Turn the piece over and, leaving ¼" seam allowance, cut away the background fabric and remove the freezer paper.

Trim ¼" inside stitching line, exposing the freezer paper.

9. Turn the piece over and admire your work. Ta Daaaa!

Getting Centered

It's usually helpful to have the centers of the blossoms marked in some way, and the easiest way to do that is to create what I call a set of "centers." First, trace all of the different blossom pieces you plan to use onto one piece of freezer paper; then iron it to another piece of freezer paper. This makes a fairly sturdy template. After cutting the templates out, find the center of each blossom by folding it in half twice, and with a thick needle, put a hole where the folds intersect.

After you've cut out your blossom pieces, before you remove the staples, orient your center template on top and with the same thick needle put a hole through them all.

PREPARING STEMS

Cutting the fabric on the straight grain works when the stems are straight. If they're curved, it's necessary to use bias strips so the stems curve without puckering. Making the stems is the same for both types of strips. Stems can be all from the same fabric, or you can make each stem different.

1. From either bias or straight-grain fabric, cut strips 1" wide by the length you need. For long strips, you may need to sew the strips together end to end.

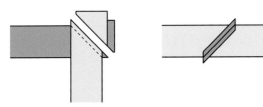

2. Fold the strips in half lengthwise, wrong sides together, and press.

3. Using a ⅛" seam allowance, sew the raw edges together.

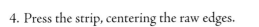

4. Press the strip, centering the raw edges.

5. Cut strips into the lengths needed and position them on the background fabric. Apply a small amount of Liquid Stitch on the background fabric where your stem is to go. Gently press the stem onto the glue and let dry. Stitch both sides of the stem in place using our narrow zigzag stitch. If the end will be covered by another appliqué piece it's not necessary to turn the edges under. However, if one end of your stem will be left uncovered, it will be necessary to turn the end under and stitch it down.

This will produce a lovely ¼" stem. If you want your stems wider, just increase the width of the strip you cut in the beginning. Remember, there is no right or wrong width for your stems.

Another way to produce perfect bias or straight-grain stems without having to sew raw edges down or risk burning your fingers is to get one of the wonderful Simplicity Bias Tape Makers. Simply cut your strips from either bias or straight grain to the width required, and then follow the manufacturer's instructions to create 12 feet of tape in a minute.

You can make single-fold bias tape in a variety of different widths with the Simplicity Bias Tape Maker.

After running the strip through the machine, it will be necessary to fold it in half lengthwise one more time and press with your iron.

Fused Machine Appliqué

Occasionally I like to use a fusible web—particularly when the piece is very, very small or when I think it would look better if fused. After trying many of the available fusible webs, the one I like best is Steam-A-Seam 2.

As with all of the other things I've mentioned, a lot depends on availability and, of course, personal preference. If you have a fusible product you've worked with and are happy with, then that's the right one for you to use. Just make sure when working with any fusible product that you read the manufacturer's recommendations for how to work with it. It's your responsibility as a consumer to read and follow the instructions if you want to get good results.

Here are step-by-step instructions for fused machine appliqué:

1. Using a pencil, trace your design onto the appropriate paper on the Steam-A-Seam 2. It's easy to figure out which is the side to draw on; try to separate the paper from the fusible web and see which one is hardest to separate. That's the one you want to draw on.

2. Roughly cut around the design, leaving about ¼" or so.

Fusible web

3. Now peel off the paper that doesn't have your design on it and finger-press the exposed fusible web to the wrong side of your appliqué fabric.

4. Cut right on the line through the paper, the fusible web, and the fabric. Do not add a seam allowance. This ensures that you'll have fusible web all the way out to the edges of your appliqué piece.

Wrong side of fabric

Keeping It All Together

Sometimes the paper doesn't stay attached to the fusible web at this point, which makes it hard to cut out your design—particularly if it's a complicated one. A little trick I use to make it stay together while I'm cutting out the design is to warm up the appliqué fabric before finger-pressing the fusible web to it. So, being careful not to put the iron anywhere near the fusible web, put the fabric right side down on your ironing board and warm up the wrong side with your iron. When you put the fusible web on the warm fabric it will hold together better while you cut out the design. Remember, do not, I repeat, do not put the iron anywhere near the fusible web at this point.

5. Remove the remaining piece of paper, making sure that the fusible web stays attached to the fabric, and position it on the right side of your background fabric. You might want to use a light box to make sure it's exactly where you want it.

6. Place the piece on your ironing board and cover with a Teflon sheet or a piece of parchment paper to protect your iron. With your iron on the cotton setting, press for 10 to15 seconds.

While browsing around on the Warm Company website (the folks who make Steam-A-Seam 2), I read their instructions for removing a piece you have fused by accident. If you apply DeSolve (a citrus-based liquid), let it sit for 15 minutes, and then wash it, you can remove fused fabric. My ironing board cover wouldn't be half as interesting if I did that!

I know that some people consider the piece done when it's been fused, but I guess I'm old fashioned. I don't think it's appliquéd until there is some thread holding the piece in place. So after fusing, I then stitch around the appliqué piece with invisible thread in the needle (again I prefer a 60/8 Universal needle) and the same stitch I use for the edge-turned appliqué.

A Practice Block

When you've made all of the necessary adjustments to your machine, it's time to start your first appliqué piece. With each of the 13 winning blocks, the order of sewing will be provided. Basically, you start at the bottom layer and work to the top. By that I mean anything that will subsequently have a piece sewn on top of it gets sewn first. For instance, in this block the stems are sewn first, because the petals and leaves that will be added later cover either part of the stem or completely cover the end of it.

So, let's choose a block to practice on. This is a favorite of mine; it was used in the "Xs and Os" quilt in my book *Machine Appliqué for the Terrified Quilter* (Martingale and Company, 2008.) My instructions are written for edge-turned invisible machine appliqué. If you prefer to fuse the pieces, the concept is the same. Simply substitute the basics for "Fused Machine Appliqué" on page 82.

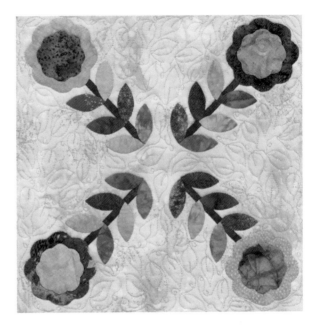

The stems don't have anything under them and are sewn first.

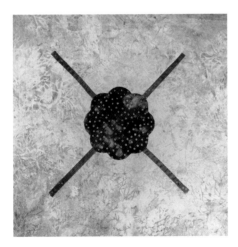

The first blossom is appliquéd over the ends of the stems.

MATERIALS

14" x 14" square of background fabric

Scraps of assorted green fabrics to total 1 fat eighth for leaves and stems

4 scraps, 4" x 4", *each* of light pink prints for flowers

4 scraps, 4" x 4", *each* of dark pink prints for flowers

Freezer paper or ½ yard of 18" fusible web

CUTTING

From the assorted green fabrics, cut 4 pieces on the straight of grain, 1" x 4½" for stems.

CREATING THE BLOCK

Refer to "Invisible Machine Appliqué" on page 75 as needed.

1. Trace and cut 24 leaf B, 4 blossom D, and 4 blossom F freezer-paper templates using the patterns on page 90.

2. Using as many different green fabrics as you wish, prepare the leaves for the block.

3. Using as many different pink (or orange, red, or purple, or whatever you choose) fabrics as you wish, prepare the blossoms for the block.

4. Make four stems using the 1" x 4½" green pieces.

5. Fold and finger-press the background in half horizontally, vertically, and diagonally, to find the center.

6. To make a placement diagram, enlarge the illustration following step 9 at right by 400% or draw a 12" square on paper, and then divide it by folding it in half vertically, horizontally, and diagonally. In the center of the square, draw a circle with a radius of 1".

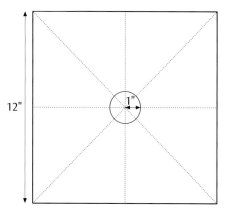

7. Put the enlarged illustration or the placement diagram on a light box and cover it with your background fabric, being careful to align the two pieces perfectly. Position one of the stem pieces on a diagonal line so that the base of it touches the center circle. When you're certain of the placement, put a small amount of Liquid Stitch on the background fabric; then gently guide the prepared stem onto the glue. Let dry. Stitch in place. Repeat with all four stems.

8. Position one blossom F at the end of a stem so that the edge of the blossom is 1" from the corner, stitch in place, and remove the freezer paper. Repeat with all four blossom F pieces. Center the blossom D pieces on top of blossom F, stitch in place, and remove the freezer paper.

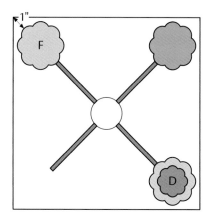

9. Position 6 leaves on each of the four stems so that the bottom two cover the raw end of the stem and the others are distributed evenly. Stitch in place and remove the freezer paper.

Enlarge 400% for placement diagram.

Ta Daaa!!! You have now successfully completed your first Rose of Sharon block.

Quilting 101

My preference, whenever possible, is to make quilts using my Reversible Quilt technique. It allows you to break the quilt down into manageable-sized pieces, it eliminates the need to baste (a great disappointment for some, I'm sure), and at no point do you have to struggle with getting half a queen- (or king- or double-) sized quilt through that little opening on your sewing machine. I'm going to show you how I put my quilt together, and then you can decide if that's the way you want to do yours. Of course if you'd rather layer and baste it the conventional way, that's entirely up to you, and I'll assume that you already know how to do that.

First let me tell you that it's not necessary to put anything fancy on the back of your quilt if you don't want to. This technique will work if you have a pieced block, a beautiful piece of fabric, or even just homely old muslin on the back. The point of making the quilt this way is to make it easier, not necessarily to make the back as beautiful as the front.

Quilting the Blocks

When you've finished the appliqué, you'll have beautiful blocks ready to be joined. First, however, you must layer and quilt them. In this book, you can see beautiful machine quilting done by Barbara Shapel, which should give you lots of ideas about how to quilt yours (see page 14). If you'd like to see more of her work, visit her website at www.barbarashapel.com

For each block, cut a square of backing and batting the same size as your appliqué block. Layer the backing, wrong side facing up, the batting, and the block with the right side facing up. Smooth out any wrinkles. Using a spray basting product (such as 505), spray baste the three layers together. Or if you prefer, layer the blocks and pin the three layers together using safety pins.

Quilt as desired. After quilting trim the blocks to 12½" x 12½". Trim evenly so the appliqué stays centered in the block.

Sashing

Sashing is used to join blocks that have already been quilted. The components are first stitched into rows, and then the rows are sewn together. You'll need sashing fabric for both the front and the back of your quilt.

I was taught to use quite narrow sashing that finishes at ⅝", and I've always called it Basic Sashing. But for many quilts, that would be out of proportion, so I'm going to show you how to make it any width you want.

1. To make wider sashing, first decide how wide you want it to be (I chose a 2" finished sashing strip for my quilt) and cut strips that size plus ½" (strips for the Rose of Sharon Block Challenge quilt were cut 2½" wide). Cut sashing strips the same size for both the front and the back of the quilt. On the sashing fabric that you've chosen for the front of your quilt, turn under ¼" toward the wrong side on one long side and press.

2. With right sides together, align the raw edge (the edge that does not have the ¼" turned under) of the sashing with the raw edge of the front of the block. Underneath, align the raw edge of the other sashing fabric with the raw edge of the block, right sides together.

3. Sew both pieces of sashing to the same block at the same time with a ¼" seam allowance. Trim the top and bottom flush with the block

4. Pin the next block to the sashing strip that doesn't have the edge turned under, with the finished back of the block pinned to the right side of the sashing strip.

5. Sew blocks together with a ¼" seam allowance.

6. Measure the distance between the resulting seam allowances and cut a strip of batting that wide. Lay the batting in the space.

7. Smooth the top sashing strip over the batting, pin in place, and hand or machine stitch the folded edge down. To hold the batting in place you must quilt the sashing strip, and I *strongly* recommend doing it as you go.

TERRE'S BORDERS (BORDERS WITHOUT SASHING)

I learned this wonderful way to add borders to an already-quilted quilt from a student in Texas. She has kindly given me permission to share it with you.

Occasionally you might want to add a border to an already-quilted quilt (think child's quilt when she/he gets a slightly larger bed and the quilt you just finished for him/her is now just a bit too small—aarrgghhhh!!!!). But, to do it with sashing just isn't going to look right. Do not despair, this technique will allow you to make your quilt larger.

1. Measure the length of the quilt through the center from top to bottom. Cut two side borders to that length from the border fabric for the front and two side borders from the fabric for the back. Piece strips together if necessary. The width is up to you.

2. Mark the centers of the borders and the quilt.

3. With right sides together, place the front border strip on the top of the quilt, matching the centers and aligning the raw edges. Pin in place. Place the back border strip, right sides together, on the back of the quilt, matching the center and aligning raw edges.

Reposition the pins. Stitch in place with a ¼" seam allowance. Remove the pins, but do not press or open the borders outward.

4. Cut two strips of batting the same length and width as the borders. Position a strip of batting right up against the raw edge of the seam allowance you just sewed, butting the edges together. Sew the batting strip to the seam allowance of the quilt using a "lycra" or "serpentine" stitch on your machine and a neutral thread color.

5. Fold both border pieces over the batting. Fuse the three layers together if using fusible batting, or pin if using non-fusible batting. (I usually sew all four borders on before doing the quilting, so I baste the raw edges together to keep them from coming unfused while the other borders are being sewn on.) Repeat the procedure for the opposite border.

6. Measure the width of your quilt through the center to cut the border strips for the top and bottom of your quilt. Repeat steps 3–5.

7. Quilt the borders as desired and sew on binding.

BASIC BINDING

This is how I bind a quilt when a single binding fabric will look good on both sides of the quilt.

1. From the width of the fabric, cut enough 2½"-wide strips to go around the quilt plus about 4" extra for joining strips and turning corners. Join the strips end to end using a diagonal seam to make a continuous strip, just like you do for sashing.

2. Fold the strip in half lengthwise, wrong sides together, and press.

3. Put the walking foot on your machine.

4. Starting at a corner and leaving a 2" tail, match the raw edges of the binding with the raw edges of the quilt. Beginning ¼" from the corner, anchor your stitches and sew the binding to the first side of the quilt with a ¼"-wide seam allowance. Stop ¼" from the corner and again anchor your stitches.

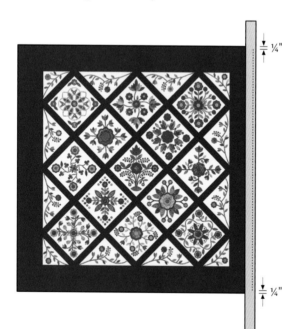

5. Remove the quilt from the machine. Draw a perpendicular line from the stitching line (A) to the fold (C). I call this the baseline.

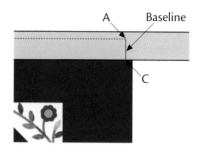

6. Measure the distance from the stitching line to the folded edge of your binding strip. It should be 1". Find the center of the baseline (it should be ½" from the folded edge and ½" from the stitching line) and make a mark. From that mark, measure ½" to the right of the baseline, and make another mark (B). Draw a line from points A and C to point B to form a triangle.

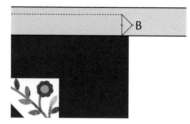

7. Fold the binding under at point B as shown. Pin in place. If you can't see the triangle you've just drawn and the folded edges are not aligned, it's folded the wrong way. Fold the quilt back out of the way and starting with the needle at point A, anchor your stitches. Then sew to point B, pivot, and sew to point C; anchor your stitches. Do not sew across the baseline.

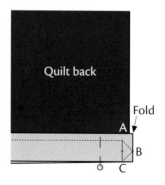

8. Remove the quilt from the machine and align the binding with the edge of the next side of the quilt.

Mark the point at which you start stitching (point D; this is under point A and ¼" from the edge). With the needle at point D, anchor your stitches, and then sew until you reach ¼" from the next corner; anchor your stitches.

9. Repeat steps 5–8 for the second and third corners. On the fourth side, sew to where you started (¼" from the end of side 4); anchor your stitches. Draw the ABC triangle as you did for the previous three corners, but instead of folding the binding under, pin it to the tail you left at the beginning, aligning the folded edges.

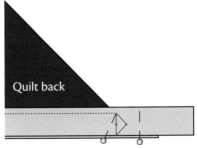

10. Sew the two sides of the triangle (from point A to B and from B to C) through both pieces of binding, thereby enclosing the ends in the corner seam.

11. Trim the corners from each triangle and turn right side out. This will give you a sewn-down mitered corner on both sides of your quilt.

12. Turn the binding to the reverse side and hand or machine stitch the folded edge to the quilt.

Rose of Sharon DVD

For those of you who like a little more visual help when learning a technique, the *Rose of Sharon* DVD is available either at your local independent quilt shop or from Nine Patch Media (www.ninepatchmedia.com). Included in the DVD is a wonderful collection of blocks (125 in all) for more Rose of Sharon possibilities. It's the perfect companion to the book.

The Patterns

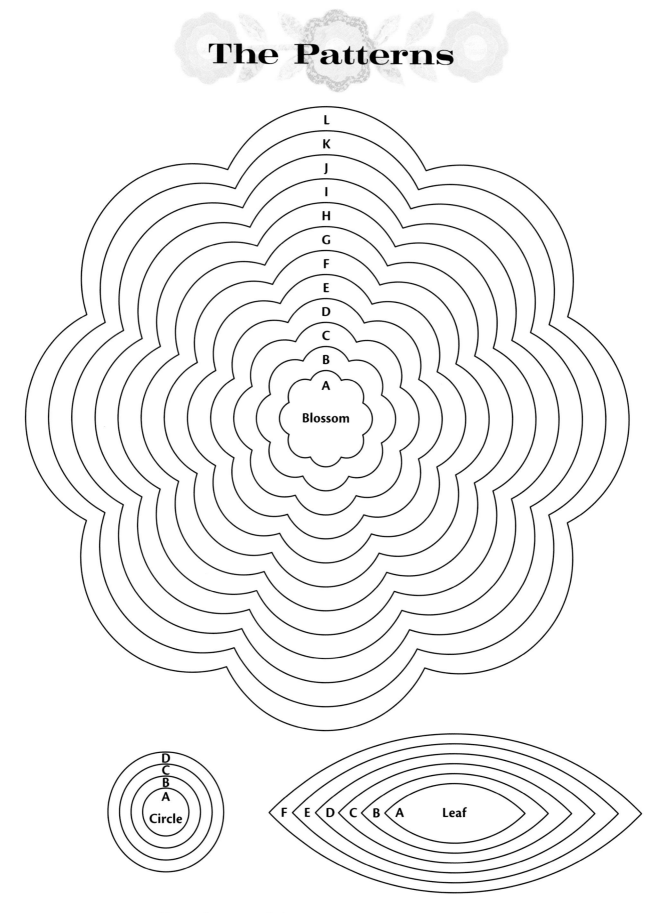

L
K
J
I
H
G
F
E
D
C
B
A

Blossom

D
C
B
A
Circle

F E D C B A   Leaf

To purchase a set of plastic templates with all these shapes,
please visit your local independent quilt shop, or visit www.ninepatchmedia.com.

Resources

Alzheimer's Art Quilt Initiative (AAQI)
www.alzquilts.org
To make a donation, participate in an auction (as a buyer or producer of quilts), or learn about the next traveling exhibit

AccuQuilt
www.accuquilt.com
A premiere line of fabric cutters and dies. Rose of Sharon custom dies for both Studio and Go! cutters

Alex Anderson and Ricky Tims
www.thequiltshow.com
Hosts and producers of the internet "TV" show *The Quilt Show*

Animas Quilts
www.animasquilts.com
Binding Miter Tool

Bernina
www.bernina.com
Sewing and embroidery machines and specialty feet

The Electric Quilt Company
www.electricquilt.com
Quilting software used to design the blocks in this book

Island Batik, Inc.
www.islandbatik.com
Manufacturers and distributors of cotton and rayon batik and hand-dyed fabrics. All of the projects in this book were made with Island Batik fabrics.

Martingale & Company
www.martingale-pub.com
Publisher of books on quilting, knitting, crochet, and more

Margaret Miller
www.millerquilts.com
Margaret is a 30-year veteran in the quilt world and has taught thousands of quilters to "reach for the unexpected" through her classes and books. She used her wonderful AnglePlay templates to create the quilt on page 73. Visit her website for more information.

Nine Patch Media
www.ninepatchmedia.com
Producers of instructional DVDs, Rose of Sharon plastic templates, precut freezer-paper Rose of Sharon templates, producers of *Rose of Sharon* instructional DVD

OESD—Oklahoma Embroidery Supply and Design
www.embroideryonline.com
Bringing you the very best embroidery software and designs. Rose of Sharon embroidery collection

Sharon Pederson
www.sharonpederson.com
Author of *Reversible Quilts: Two at a Time* (2002), *More Reversible Quilts* (2004), *Sensational Sashiko: Japanese Appliqué and Quilting by Machine* (2005), *Color for the Terrified Quilter* (2007), *Machine Appliqué for the Terrified Quilter* (2008), all from Martingale & Company

Pellon
www.pellon.com
Producers of 13 quality quilt batting products under the name "Legacy"

Barbara Shapel
www.barbarashapel.com
An award-winning quilter who has many first-place and Best of Show ribbons on her quilts, Barbara quilted "Roses of Remembrance" on page 14. Visit her website to see more of her work.

Rainy Day Quilts
www.rainydayquilts.com
Long-arm quilting by Wanda Rains

The Warm Company
www.warmcompany.com
Steam-A-Seam 2

Challenge Fabrics
from Island Batik, Inc.

All of the fabrics in this book came from the Rose of Sharon line from Island Batik, Inc. If by chance your fabric store does not carry a specific fabric, they can use the numbers below for ordering. As with most batiks, colors shift from spot to spot, so don't be surprised if the photos in this book don't match the samples below.

BLOSSOMS, LEAVES, STEMS, AND CIRCLES

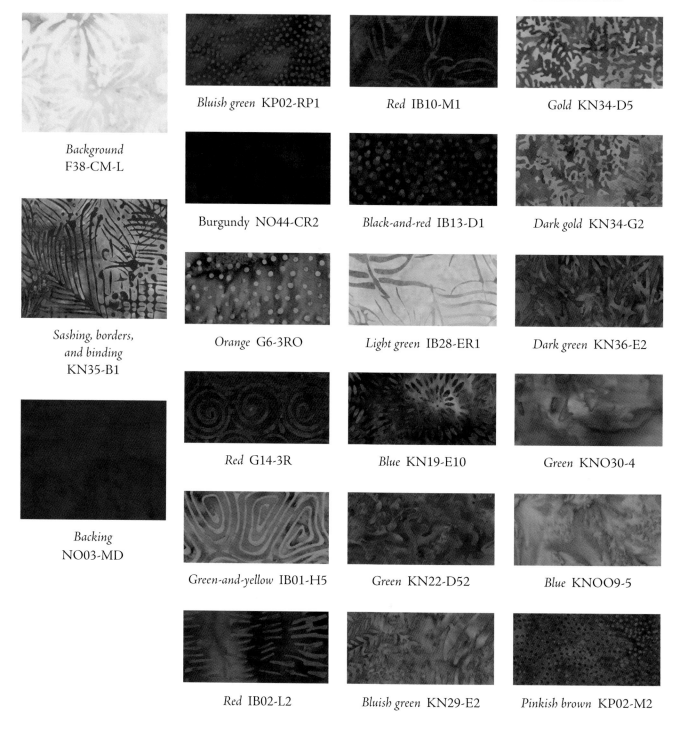

Background
F38-CM-L

Sashing, borders,
and binding
KN35-B1

Backing
NO03-MD

Bluish green KP02-RP1

Red IB10-M1

Gold KN34-D5

Burgundy NO44-CR2

Black-and-red IB13-D1

Dark gold KN34-G2

Orange G6-3RO

Light green IB28-ER1

Dark green KN36-E2

Red G14-3R

Blue KN19-E10

Green KNO30-4

Green-and-yellow IB01-H5

Green KN22-D52

Blue KNOO9-5

Red IB02-L2

Bluish green KN29-E2

Pinkish brown KP02-M2

Rose of Sharon
EQ6 Block Challenge Winners

Kari Bauer, Oak Park, Illinois, USA
Block 13

Pat Daniels, Winnipeg, Manitoba, Canada
Block 11

Jo Moury, Haymarket, Virginia, USA
Block 6

Judy Best, London, Ontario, Canada
Block 2

Candace Door, Sydney, Nebraska, USA
Block 10

Suzy Prickett, Melbourne, Florida, USA
Block 8

Claudia Chang, Taipei, Taiwan
Block 12

Dianne Gronfors, Bracebridge, Ontario,
Canada
Block 3

Rebekah Reinheimer, Jerusalem, Israel
Block 7

Leslie Collins, El Granada, California,
USA
Block 5

Simonetta Marini, San Giovanni,
Persiceto, Bologna, Italy
Block 1

Barb Vlack, Saint Charles, Illinois, USA
Block 9

Acknowledgments

I've always enjoyed and appreciated the help of countless family members, friends, and students while writing books, but with this book the number of people who contributed has grown enormously. I feel like the single person at the top of a human pyramid, standing on the shoulders of the many who made it possible.

First, I want to thank the partners in The Rose of Sharon Project—who all enthusiastically jumped on board at the very beginning—Penny McMorris at the Electric Quilt Company; Adam and Moira Dewar at Island Batik; Alex Anderson and Ricky Tims of *The Quilt Show*; H. D. Wilbanks Jr. and Darlene Christopherson at Pellon; Andrea Ronning of AccuQuilt; Tom Wierzbicki and Mary Green at Martingale & Company; Kim Goodwin of Oklahoma Embroidery Supply and Design; Jeanne C. Delpit, Gail Wheeler, and Leslie A. Brown at Bernina of America; Barbara Shapel; and of course my partners at Nine Patch Media, Elizabeth Phillips and Chris Manuel.

In truth Elizabeth and Chris both should have their names on the cover, as their contributions were immense.

To Ami Sims—you are an inspiration!

To my friends and great color consultants Ionne McCauley and Gladys Love—you're the best rescue team ever—thanks for your valuable (and cheerful) input.

For the 11th hour quilting and binding, my thanks to Coreen Zerr.

To Gail MacRae—your edge-turned blossoms are the best!

As always, many thanks to the talented group at Martingale & Company—to Mary, Stan, Karen, Laurel, Brent, Regina, and a particularly huge thank-you to my technical editor Robin Strobel who, with great patience and humor, walked me through the minefield of triangles and percentages.

And, to our designers—to the many who entered the Rose of Sharon Block Challenge and sent in the amazing blocks you now see in this book—many thanks for sharing your creativity with us all.

Last, but never least, to my patient, funny, supportive, errand-running, dinner-reservation-making husband, Sy, thank you for being there always.

About the Author

Sharon Pederson is a popular teacher around the world. While her home base is on Canada's beautiful Vancouver Island, she has taught at major conferences and for guilds all over North America. She has also had the pleasure of teaching in England, Scotland, Wales, South Africa, Dubai, Hawaii, and on four quilt cruises. A quilting tour of Japan, and an exciting trip to Morocco and Spain with Jim West of Sew Many Places, are also in the works.

Her love of teaching is evident in all of her classes, where her students acquire not only quilting skills but also a level of confidence that has them tackling more ambitious projects than they had previously thought possible. But, before you come to the conclusion that it is work, work, work, this acquisition of skills is done with a hearty dose of humor. Sharon believes that students learn more if they are having a good time and her goal is to provide both the skills and the fun.

Along with her two partners, Elizabeth Phillips and Chris Manuel, she has also managed to produce 16 DVD titles in between writing books and traveling to teach.

What does she do in her spare time? She reads, cooks, goes for long walks on her beloved Saratoga Beach, and watches movies with her best friend (and husband) Sy.

There's More Online!

Please visit www.sharonpederson.com, which includes Sharon's very entertaining blog, or www.ninepatchmedia.com, where you can see all of the latest DVD titles. And be sure to sign up for her Rose of Sharon Yahoo Group (available on her website).

You might also enjoy these other fine titles from

Martingale & Company